"I literally grew up with Andrea—in front of and behind the camera. Her memoir perfectly captures the funny, smart, inspiring, raw, and honest heart of my dearest friend."
    —**Candace Cameron Bure**

"I could not be more proud of my friend and fellow 'She-Wolf.' She is truly one of the most genuine, loving people I know. Her struggles with anxiety and depression, and how she broke through, are so incredibly relatable. As someone who has fought those demons myself, I found her candor both poignant and funny. A great read from a multitalented actress, author, and comedienne! The millions of fans who love her will not be disappointed!"
    —**Jodie Sweetin**

"Andrea is brave, open, and so very human. Between the laughs, her memoir highlights her imperfections and struggles, and her journey to acceptance. Her fans will find stories about their favorite girl next-door, and readers will be inspired to embrace their own uniqueness and to keep looking forward with humor and strength."
    —**Tan France,** *Queer Eye,* and author of *Naturally Tan*

"Andrea Barber writes with equal parts humor and raw honesty. Her willingness to share her struggles along with her joys makes her incredibly relatable. Tackling motherhood, divorce, mental illness, careers, aging, and everything in between, makes *Full Circle* a perfect read for anyone navigating their own troubles. This book makes you realize you are not alone and that there are many bright days ahead. It leaves the reader with hope."
    —**Kara Goucher,** two-time Olympian
        and world champion runner

"Stepping on a stage and playing a part is a craft that can be honed. Opening up and sharing your true self with the world takes a courage that can't be taught. In *Full Circle*, Andrea Barber pulls back the curtains and courageously shares her story in a way that's authentic, real, and raw. She'll always be thought of as Kimmy Gibbler, but after *Full Circle* she'll forever be loved for being authentically Andrea Barber."

—**Desiree Linden,** Olympic athlete and winner of the 2018 Boson Marathon

"In this very funny, relatable, and refreshingly candid memoir, Andrea Barber does something brave: she gracefully shares her struggles behind her celebrity—her anxiety, her life as a single working mom, and her hard-won transformation—and in the process makes us see what's possible in our own lives. Prepare to be entertained and inspired."

—**Lori Gottlieb,** *New York Times* bestselling author of *Maybe You Should Talk to Someone: A Therapist, Her Therapist, and Our Lives Revealed*

"I love this book for so many reasons. Andrea Barber's unflinching, candid expression of painful realities creates an authenticity that immediately connects the reader to her journey. She speaks from her heart with language that every mom, every *person*, can relate to. In doing so, she normalizes anxiety, depression, panic, shame, grief, therapy, and medication, and singlehandedly destigmatizes the high distress that is so often associated with new motherhood. Wonderfully written, her memoir takes us through her unique life experiences all the way to her impressive strategies for coping and building resilience.

—**Karen Kleiman,** founder, The Postpartum Stress Center, and author of Good Moms Have Scary Thoughts

Full Circle

From Hollywood
to Real Life and
Back Again

Andrea Barber

CITADEL PRESS
Kensington Publishing Corp.
www.kensingtonbooks.com

CITADEL PRESS BOOKS are published by

Kensington Publishing Corp.
119 West 40th Street
New York, NY 10018

Copyright © 2019 Andrea Barber

All rights reserved. No part of this book may be reproduced in any form or by any means without the prior written consent of the publisher, excepting brief quotes used in reviews.

All Kensington titles, imprints, and distributed lines are available at special quantity discounts for bulk purchases for sales promotions, premiums, fund-raising, educational, or institutional use.

Special book excerpts or customized printings can also be created to fit specific needs. For details, write or phone the office of the Kensington sales manager: Kensington Publishing Corp., 119 West 40th Street, New York, NY 10018, attn: Sales Department; phone 1-800-221-2647.

CITADEL PRESS and the Citadel logo are Reg. U.S. Pat. & TM Off.

ISBN-13: 978-0-8065-3989-8
ISBN-10: 0-8065-3989-5

ISBN-13: 978-0-8065-4088-7 (hardcover, signed edition)
ISBN-10: 0-8065-4088-5 (hardcover, signed edition)

First Citadel hardcover printing: December 2019
First Citadel trade paperback edition: November 2020

10 9 8 7 6 5 4 3 2 1

Printed in the United States of America

Electronic edition:

ISBN-13: 978-0-8065-3990-4 (e-book)
ISBN-10: 0-8065-3990-9 (e-book)

To my mom, Sherry Barber.

Everything that is good about me comes from you.
From your capacity to love to your ability to pour your heart
onto the page . . . thank you. I love you.

CONTENTS

CHAPTER ONE
Not Me

"WE'RE ROLLING!"

Cue panic. My world suddenly narrows to the size of a pinhole. I can't think about anything except the spinning insecurities swirling in my head. *Can I do this . . . again?*

The year is 2015, and it's been exactly twenty years since I've last stepped into a scene as one of television's most iconic characters, Kimmy Gibbler. My heart feels as though it's beating outside of my chest, and I can't seem to catch my breath no matter how hard I try. My head is pounding with loud thoughts—none of which include the lines I'm minutes away from having to deliver.

I've been on television for over thirty-five years, and I still feel uncomfortable calling myself a "celebrity." I am an introverted, anxious, quiet person who plays a very extroverted, confident, loud character on television. And often, during the eight-year run of *Full House*, I would go to the bathroom before tapings to vomit.

At the time, I thought getting sick before performing was

something everyone did. I didn't realize that these were the first signs of a lifelong battle with anxiety and depression, something I would hate about myself for years to come. At the time I was just a kid, just playing a role.

The interesting thing about acting, though, is that it always seems to counteract those anxious feelings that I struggle with so much. I love the thrill of getting into character. I love making people laugh. The camera turns on, and my muscle memory takes over. The stress melts away when the director yells "Action!" and, for a few minutes, I get to be someone else. I get to play this fiercely confident character who's outlandish and zany but *owns* everything about herself. She isn't plagued with spiraling doubts and worries. I get to be . . . well, Not Me. And then the audience claps and hollers for this Not Me, this other person who I created. It's a liberating feeling.

After *Full House* ended, I basically quit Hollywood. I went to college, lived abroad, married my boyfriend, had kids, got walloped by debilitating depression and anxiety, and went through a divorce. In short, I got lost. And then I found my way back. Literally. I found my way back to the Tanner family home on the spin-off series *Fuller House*. How's that for going full circle?

I've played a weird but bold character my entire life, and now I want you to know me. *All* of me. The good, the bad, and especially the strange. I have the unique perspective of not only having been a child actor, but then returning to *that same character* as an adult after twenty years away from her, and from showbiz as a whole. I can tell you what it's like to survive Hollywood, both as a child and as an adult, and come out the other side as a relatively normal person. People think celebrities live these very different lives. Especially with the rise of social media, celebrity lives become celebrity highlight reels. You don't ever really see that person binge-eating cake, stewing over a nasty comment (or ten) someone left on their Instagram page, fighting with her boyfriend, or crying herself to sleep. You only see the staged snapshots of moments intended to create an illusion of perfection. But we're really not that different. Just because you don't see those moments of struggle doesn't mean they don't happen.

I feel like many celebrity books are how-to books—*be like me*! Let me emphasize: THIS IS NOT A HOW-TO BOOK. This is an honest look at my life, the highs and the lows, my successes and failures. I am also writing this book to give fans—many of whom have been extremely loyal for over thirty years—a behind-the-scenes view of the show that redefined the traditional family on TV. I've got so much to share, especially with *Fuller House* adding a new chapter to the *Full House* story.

I am here to talk about my anxiety and depression. Because, dammit, it's critical that we talk about it. It's important to let each other know that we're not alone. It's important to let others know what it's like living with anxiety and depression every day. Lots of things—my divorce, my depression, my anxiety—I kept secret even from my close friends for years because I was ashamed. I wanted to write this book so I could share what I've kept inside of me for *so* long. We can create a culture of acceptance and healing. We just need to stop being silent about it. We need to speak up.

I received a direct message on Instagram from a fan not long ago. She wrote, "Growing up, I found your character unique . . . not because she had a personality that stands out from 'normal' people, but because she was confident about it. Growing up, I didn't know that it was possible to be different and confident, so I was forcing myself to be like everyone else . . . [I] stopped living my life the way I do in private. Thank you for showing confidence in your eyes, it spoke to me." I relate *so* much to what this fan writes. Who among us hasn't experienced self-doubt and wanting to fit in? It took me a long time, well into my adult years, before I felt as confident as Kimmy is.

I always thought a memoir was something you write at the end of your life, to reflect back on lessons learned and a life well lived. I think age forty-three is terribly young to be reflecting on my life—especially when I hopefully haven't even finished living half my life yet! But in the past few years, I've realized that I suddenly have a sizeable audience wanting to listen. I might make a difference *now* if I write about my life now. So I'm jumping in headfirst.

I'm writing this book because I have never really been able to express myself in an honest and open way before. In a way, I'm a terrible celebrity. I hate giving interviews and avoid seeking out publicity opportunities. There is a lot that people don't know about me because I've never really put it out there before. I am a private person who regularly performs on a very public stage. In real life, I couldn't be *less* like Kimmy Gibbler.

To fans, I've always been synonymous with my character, since most people don't know me in any other role. But now, I want you to accept the *real* me . . . and the fact that I'm nothing like I appear on TV. To know me is to realize that I am very flawed, and I have many shortcomings and insecurities. By sharing them with you, you may recognize things in yourself, and discover that you and I are not so unalike after all. For once, it will be nice to share Andrea with the world.

Most of all, I want to form a human connection with you. I've lived inside your TV screens, inside your homes, for over thirty years now; it's time we really get to know each other. I hope, by sharing my story with you, you will understand the person behind Kimmy Gibbler. The girl who never felt comfortable in her own skin but had to act otherwise in front of cameras. The college student who found life outside of Hollywood, but always stayed close with her *Full House* family. The woman who faced life's challenges, found her inner strength, rebooted, and became that confident person in a leading role you see on camera. The mom who now watches *Full* and *Fuller House* with her own kids and laughs at how ridiculous she looked as a teenager.

This is me. All of me. I hope you'll find a little of yourself here, too.

CHAPTER TWO
Beginnings

PEOPLE ARE ALWAYS ASKING ME, "How did you get into acting?"

My answer: "By accident."

That's only half true. The longer answer is that I grew up doing community theater with my family. The five of us—my mom, my dad, my two brothers, and I—each had a role in the local production of *A Christmas Carol* every December. It was a family affair—not your typical family hobby, I realize, especially considering *no one* in my family was an aspiring actor. My dad was an attorney. My mom was a second grade teacher. But they loved participating in local theater, so we did it as a family.

I landed my *very first* role at the age of six months as the Baby Jesus in our church's live nativity performance. My mom and dad were Mary and Joseph. Yeah, they started me out early, but that was probably the easiest role I ever had. (I think I might have even slept through part of it!)

It was during one of these Barber family local plays that an actors' strike was occurring in Hollywood. It left performers eager to keep honing their skills by turning to local theater, so a number of young working actors took part in that same play: *The King and I* at La Mirada Theatre for the Performing Arts— a venue anyone would be pleased to have on their résumé. During rehearsals, the moms would chat, and one professional kid actor's mom encouraged my mom to call Judy Savage, her child's agent.

"She understands about being a mom," the woman said. "She's not a piranha." Before my mom got around to calling, the other mom had already mentioned me, and Judy was calling *us,* inviting me to her office for an interview. And when Judy found out I had two older brothers, she asked my mom to bring them, too. She told us that girls were always more interested in acting, so boys weren't as plentiful on the audition circuit. My parents, being somewhat clueless and mostly curious, drove me and my brothers, Darin and Justin, out to Judy's office on a whim.

There, Judy taught us how to "slate." Slating is an acting term used for on-camera auditions. You state your name, your age (if you're a child), and the agent who sent you to the audition before you start the scene. This goes on tape for the casting director's reference. After demonstrating, Judy asked us to show her how we slate. My brothers performed this task flawlessly. When it was my turn, I confidently declared, "My name is Andrea Barber, I'm four years old, and I'm from the AVERAGE Agency!"

Judy signed all three of us on the spot. (And we still keep in touch today.)

And that, my friends, is the official story of "how I started acting."

From then on, my life has been anything but average. I grew up—literally *grew up*—on television. After the community theater years, I got my first big TV break at age five with a commercial for Velveeta cheese, charming people across America with my messy pigtails and toothless smile. I don't remember much from that job, just a lot of very bright lights. I don't even remember if I ate the cheese, to be honest. I was a cute kid with a big personality, but looking back at the VHS (!) tapes now, I can see just how precocious I was. I also see it in my daughter, which both delights and terrifies me.

I did other commercials, mostly for toys and McDonald's. This was the 1980s, long before the invention of TiVo or DVR. Commercials mattered! Commercials were to be watched, not simply fast-forwarded through or used as a bathroom break. They were actually part of the TV-viewing experience, so having commercials on your résumé meant a lot back then.

I remember doing a commercial for Intellivision (a game console back in the '80s—kind of like Xbox waaaaay before Xbox) where I had to play a game of Dungeons & Dragons. This was actually a good fit for me, because I had spent hours watching my own brothers play Intellivision. So I felt well prepared for this role. My brother in the commercial was played by Henry Thomas, who also happened to be the kid from *E.T. the Extra-Terrestrial*—which had recently been released and become an instant blockbuster. I remember being confused that everyone was super excited that Henry was on set; I hadn't seen the movie yet.

"How was it working with the kid from *E.T.*?" someone asked. I shrugged and said, "I don't know. He had a cold that day; he did the best he could with his lines." It's hard to be a fangirl when you don't recognize the star.

Another commercial I remember shooting was for Sunsweet prunes. Oh dear. I remember this one especially because I didn't actually love prunes. Does any kid? Prunes were something your mom made you eat when you couldn't poop! But here I was making a commercial for them, and I had to eat the prunes—*every single take.*

Before you panic at the outcome of this scenario, I'll let you in on a little Hollywood trick: spit buckets. The prop master always has a spit bucket nearby so the actor doesn't have to eat an abnormal amount of food each take and get sick to her stomach. And such was the case with my prune commercial. I had one such bucket underneath my chair, and I spat out each prune as soon as the director yelled, "Cut!" But that still meant I had to keep the prunes in my mouth and chew for several seconds until he got the shot. UGH. To this day, I hate prunes. Clearly, I am a terrible promoter for this fruit!

My brothers Darin and Justin had a good amount of success in the acting world, doing commercials for "Sip Ups" drinks and making an appearance on *General Hospital* (no scenes with John Stamos as Blackie, though!). When they got to high school, they decided they would rather play indoor volleyball than drive to Hollywood for auditions. Acting can be tedious, going from audition to audition and getting rejection after rejection. But volleyball provided instant gratification from winning a game or even just nailing a serve. I don't think they ever thought twice about hanging up their acting hats.

So that just left me with acting as a hobby. But at least in some ways, I was still a normal kid, with normal, little-kid oddities. I was convinced I wanted to be a bird someday. Literally. I did not comprehend that this was not possible. I talked to birds. I sat on the train next to the window with bird poop on purpose—not exaggerating. I was completely obsessed with being a bird. (I have never discussed this with my therapist, and now I wonder what she would say about it.) In first grade, we were assigned to write about what we wanted to be when we grew up. I wrote about being a bird. My teacher lectured me about taking the assignment seriously! Ummm . . . I *was* being serious, Ms. Camp.

Even when I wasn't onstage or in front of the camera, I was often acting and playing pretend. We had a large closet in our house my mom called "The Etc. Room." It's where *everything else* went: extra toilet paper, folding chairs, etcetera. It was akin to the junk drawer that most people have, but we had a whole room. I spent hours in that Etc. Room. Every day after school, I would write little assignments and pretend I was a teacher, then grade those assignments with a red crayon. I wrote fictional stories about little girls. I even created my own bookbindings with Scotch tape. I had lots of friends as a kid, but I was very happy with just me and my imagination.

At age six, I landed my first major, steady gig: playing Carrie Brady, the firstborn child of the beloved Roman Brady and Anna DiMera on the soap opera *Days of Our Lives*. I have discovered that people fall into one of three camps:

1. You have never watched soap operas.
2. You were an avid watcher of *DOOL* and are amazed

to discover that there was a different Carrie Brady before Christie Clark.

3. You are a devout *DOOL* fan, and you not only remember me as Carrie Brady, but you also remember when Roman Brady snuck into the Salem Hospital disguised as Santa Claus (in order to evade his archnemesis, the evil Stefano DiMera) to visit Carrie, who was in a coma after she slipped on ice and hit her head. Then he read her the story of Baby Jesus, during which time Carrie miraculously awoke from her coma to see her father sobbing over her bed. (God, I love soap operas!)

So that was my first big role. I worked on *Days of Our Lives* for three and a half years. I started the show on my sixth birthday—the actual day!—and the producers brought out a cake in the shape of a barber pole. This is what you remember about Hollywood from back when you were just six years old: cake. I had no complaints.

DOOL is where I learned how to memorize lots and lots of new dialogue daily—soap operas shoot one new episode *every day*—and how to cry on command. Soap operas are like boot camp for actors: they work you hard for very long hours, but by the end you have honed your acting skills quite sharply. Full disclosure: I stole this analogy from John Brotherton, who plays D.J.'s ex-love interest Matt on *Fuller House*. I don't know how I cried on command at such a young age; everyone seemed amazed. I just pretended to be in the moment (My father was brainwashed and killed by Stefano? Sure, that *is* sad), and the tears came.

The true genius was Deidre Hall, who played my stepmother, Marlena. Not only could she cry on command, she could produce tears specifically from the downstage eye, i.e. the one closest to the camera. And she never messed up her flawless makeup. Now THAT is talent!

One year, Wayne Northrop, who played my father, Roman, filled our car with inflated balloons as my birthday surprise. It was awesome! My parents were less enthusiastic. I didn't want to pop any, but of course my mom deflated them so we could safely drive home on the freeway. My mom and I both remember Wayne's patience and kindness. During a luncheon at a big hotel for *DOOL* fans, I kept pestering him to play with me; I was only seven, after all. Deidre was at the mic, talking to fans about not photographing the actors while they ate, and I entertained myself by reaching over to "honk honk" Wayne's nose. He played along and never showed irritation. He was a great father figure, both on- and offstage.

My journey as a soap opera star came to a screeching halt when I was nine years old. Now I'm *sure* this is merely a coincidence, but I'll mention it anyway: The production schedule changed suddenly, and I was needed on a week that I was originally scheduled to have off. My family had long-standing plans, as we did every Easter week, to be in Mammoth Lakes, a popular ski resort in central California. The producers insisted I needed to be at the studio; my dad refused to back down. We had cleared my schedule and booked this family trip months in advance. Although my parents loved acting, it was always about the fun of acting, never the business. For my entire career, my parents were dead set on my life being centered around my home, my family, my school—all the "real" stuff. Not Hollywood. To rearrange the trip so that a parent and I could suddenly be on set would have upset the entire family's vacation. So my dad said no. And we went to Mammoth.

The next week, the *DOOL* producers called my parents to regretfully inform them that the writers had decided they needed a "teenage summer romance" storyline, and they would be aging my character to be a teenager. So one day, young Carrie (me) went upstairs to play with her toys, and came back downstairs the next day as a teenager (Christie Clark). Oh, soap operas. Fired at age nine! That's Hollywood. I wasn't sad; I was a fourth grader, and this was just a hobby. My identity and happiness weren't—and never have been—tied up in my successes in Hollywood. It wasn't personal, and it wasn't about my talent or lack thereof. I also felt just as fulfilled being a regular nine-year-old at school and being a Girl Scout. Back then, I didn't consider success on a soap opera as the end-all, be-all of happiness. I had equal amounts of fun going camping with my troop.

My journey as a child actor was an uncomplicated one because there simply weren't as many child actors in the 1980s as there are now (read: less competition), and acting came very naturally to me. It was my hobby. I never viewed it as a career, or a means to make money, or a way to be famous. Now, it's true that all of that ended up happening anyway. But at the time, it was simply my after-school sport. The fact that it became my career and changed my life was . . . luck? Fate? I'm going with luck. *Really* good luck.

CHAPTER THREE

Growing Up Gibbler

ONE QUESTION I GET ASKED A LOT is, "What was it like auditioning for *Full House*?" I'll be honest: I don't remember. First of all, I was ten years old, so this was thirty-some years ago. Second, it was just one more in a myriad of auditions that I did on the weekly circuit. It's not like I went into it thinking, "OMG! I'm auditioning for the mega cult-hit *Full House*! Pressure!" There *was* no *Full House* yet. This could have easily just been another show that flopped. No one could have predicted the success of a show about three men trying to raise three girls . . . with the wacky neighbor girl frequently popping in to deliver zingers. To me, it was just another audition, just another guest appearance. Lather, rinse, repeat.

People do seem tickled when I tell them that I auditioned for the role of D.J. first, didn't get that part (obviously), and then got called back to read for the role of the pesky neighbor. Again, this isn't uncommon in Hollywood. It's not some big dis or insult. It's common to read for a role, not get it, and then be asked to come back and read for a different part. It doesn't mean you're a terrible actor; it just means you weren't the right fit for that particular role. If anything, this particular casting choice was a reflection of my looks: awkward and gangly. For an offbeat character, this was perfect. And the good news was that the producers remembered my audition enough to ask me to come back and read for Kimmy Gibbler. Yay, I was memorable! That's what you want in Hollywood. And the rest, as they say, is history.

The part of Kimmy Gibbler was supposed to be a onetime appearance, which turned into five episodes of season one, which turned into eight years of my life. I think the audience responded to Kimmy with a love-hate attitude: Either you loved her or you couldn't stand her. Kimmy is bold and confident, abrasive and overly honest, zany and quirky. She marches to the beat of her own drum. She barges through the back kitchen door unannounced and has all the confidence in the world, no matter what anyone has to say about her.

It was the kind of confidence that both inspired me and left me awestruck. Who *was* this character? I couldn't have been more different from Kimmy Gibbler. I was introverted, quiet, shy, and decidedly *unconfident*. Kimmy was the breathing, walking definition of "extrovert." Somehow, I managed to still play this character despite our differences, although I think it took me a few years before I really embraced her and let go of my preteen insecurities.

I spent a long time—most of the eight years, actually—hating my wardrobe. Kimmy's clothing choices were not trendy or inspiring, to say the least. The odd pairings of colors and patterns and neon *everything* was oftentimes an eyesore or the butt of another joke. I think, had I been a lot older, this wouldn't have been such a big deal. But as a prepubescent tween growing into her teenage years, this felt like social suicide. I knew I was just playing a character, but I dreaded fittings and having to put on clothing that made me feel even more awkward on the outside than I already felt on the inside. I was never the type of teenager who wore a lot of makeup or fussed with her hair too much. In fact, even to this day, the messy bun is my go-to look. So I guess it isn't surprising that costume fittings and staring at myself for hours in the makeup chair made me hyperaware of my appearance.

I was also a quiet people-pleaser, so I rarely, if ever, spoke up if I felt uncomfortable in the wardrobe. I wanted to be a "good" actor and go with the flow. I didn't want to voice my negative opinions and risk ruffling any feathers. So I grinned and endured it and wore costumes that I loathed. Our costumer, Roberta, was a wonderful and talented woman who had a bit of an eccentric style herself, and I loved her. She never made me feel uncomfortable or pressured me to wear the wacky costumes. It was my internal insecurities—my inability to speak up and use my voice—that was the problem.

The other girls on the show got to wear cute, age-appropriate clothing, and I envied them. At the end of every season, the wardrobe department would ask us if we wanted to take home any of the clothes we wore that season (as growing kids, we would outgrow them by the next season, so rather than let them go to waste, they let us keep the clothes). I dejectedly watched as the other girls combed through their piles of stylish clothes. I rarely, if ever, took home any of Kimmy's clothes. Maybe a pair of inoffensive pants, but that's it.

I know these are seriously first-world problems: *Boo hoo, I hated the clothes I wore on my hit TV show!* But remembering it all now, this experience speaks to my growing insecurities as a child and how *not* speaking up to voice my concerns made me feel worse in the long run. Speaking up and saying, "This particular outfit makes me uncomfortable, but maybe we can find something together that is unique and funny but still within my comfort zone," would have gone a long way toward bolstering my confidence. Swallowing my voice and feelings just made me feel terrible.

It's a lesson I've taken with me into my adult life. On *Fuller House*, I learned to speak up, respectfully but honestly. Our costumer on the show, Mary Kate, and I developed a rapport and mutual respect. She knew what made me comfortable versus what made me uncomfortable, and she never forced me to wear anything that I truly felt awful wearing. And in return, I was willing to try on *any* combination of crazy clothes to let her experiment and play with styles until we found something that we both loved. The result was a fun, unique, stylish wardrobe that helped me get into character, but also gave me the confidence to be Kimmy Gibbler. It was a win-win.

One of our first inspirations was the character Carrie Bradshaw from *Sex and the City*, who is quirky but fashionable, daring, and confident. Mary Kate would pair a floral blouse with a black-and-white polka-dot skirt (something I would normally never do or think of), yet somehow it *worked* and looked trendy. She was a master at finding quirky items, many of which came from Etsy or ModCloth. One of the first photo stills that was released before season one had a picture of Kimmy in a cat kimono, and that's all anyone could talk about on social media. The cat kimono broke the Internet.

Becoming close to the costumers on the show is a given (Hello, don't mind me as I undress in front of you during our weekly fittings!), but that closeness extends all across the stage, from crew to cast and beyond. The cast speaks often and openly about how close we all are, a true second family for each of us, and it all began in those early seasons of *Full House*. It was truly a joy to come to work every day. For years during and after *Full House*, people always asked me, "What's it like on set?" My answer was always the same: Fun! I don't know any other word to describe it. There was always a lot of laughter on set. Bob Saget and Dave Coulier were (still are) professional comedians, so jokes were always flying. They kept them pretty PG-rated when the kids were around, but every once in a while you would see our moms offstage sitting in the bleachers, which were otherwise empty on rehearsal days, wagging a warning finger at Bob or Dave or calling out from backstage, "Bob!"

The three men on *Full House*—Bob, Dave, and John—were experts at providing comic relief during long workdays. One pre-tape night I will never forget was during the "Five's A Crowd" episode in season five. Danny, Jesse, and Joey show up unannounced to D.J.'s date at the drive-in, fearing that her "bad boy" date Pete was solely interested in scoring with D.J. The scene opens with the three men walking around the van, attempting to peek inside. For some reason, the guys had to do this scene over and over and over; it was getting late, and everyone was ready to go home, but the director couldn't get the shot just right. Frustrating for all. So how did Bob, Dave, and John respond? They pulled their tuxedo pants down *and entered the scene with their pants around their ankles.* Boxer shorts on full display, the guys couldn't even pretend to keep a straight face! Our director, Joel Zwick, just laughed and shook his head. Our moms, watching from the studio audience, rolled their eyes. Classic Bob, Dave, and John. If their goal was to break the tension on the set, they achieved just that.

One time, the horsing around got to be a little too much. There was more joking than working, and Joel had just had it. He yelled from his director's chair, "Everyone in the green-room! Now!"

Oh boy. Joel was tiny, but *man* could he get angry and loud when he needed to. We marched up to the greenroom, fearing the lecture we were about to endure. But who trailed right behind us into the greenroom? Little toddlers Mary-Kate and Ashley Olsen, wide-eyed and innocent. They were just following the cast like everyone else! So our tongue-lashing from a steaming Joel was quickly downgraded to a stern warning, with Joel knowing he couldn't use the choice words I'm sure were running through his head. (These stories are legendary among the cast.)

John Stamos was, of course, the heartthrob on set, although none of us kids thought of him that way. Sure, the audience would scream the loudest when his name was called during introductions on tape night (and again during curtain call). But he always just felt like, well, the *cool uncle* on set. I guess life imitates art, after all. But you have to remember that I was only ten years old when I first met John. I was too young to have ever watched him on *General Hospital*, where he earned his Blackie fame. He was just a really nice dude to me. By the time I was old enough to think boys were cute, I knew John too well. He wasn't cute, he was just John—my *good friend* John. Reporters ask all the time now, "Did you ever have a crush on John Stamos?" and Candace, Jodie, and I hate it when this question pops up. NO! *Stoppit!* That's just weird. No one has a crush on their uncle, am I right? So no, I never found him attractive in the "OMG-Joey-McIntyre-makes-my-heart-stop!" kind of way. But as an adult now who is faced daily with her own signs of aging, I can look at John and truly appreciate his beauty, his amazing jawline, and his flawless skin. I still want to know his skin-care routine. Funny fact: He has always called me "Kimmy Gibbler" in real life. I chuckle now because back in the day, he probably simply didn't remember my real name. (I wasn't a full-time cast member back then.) But now he does it as a true joke. Sometimes he'll slip and refer to me as "Andrea," but he usually catches himself and resumes calling me "Kimmy" or simply "Gibbler," even in texts and emails.

Lori Loughlin was, and still is, absolutely 100 percent as lovely and sweet as she seems. We've all seen her vilified in the news amidst the college admissions scandal, and it hurts my heart every time I see a new headline, because those headlines *do not* paint a complete (or even accurate) picture of who she is. While I don't know enough about the case specifically to comment on it one way or another, I do agree with what our friend Candace said at the Kids' Choice Awards. Family is family, and I maintain my love for Lori.

Lori is one of the kindest people I've ever met. She gets along with everyone. People are drawn to her. She is also probably the most beautiful person I've ever met who never draws attention to her beauty. In that sense, I call her an effortless beauty because, unlike a lot of celebrities, she never feels the need to point it out. She is one of the least affected, most humble people you will ever meet. And she has a laugh that is utterly contagious! Lori was definitely like the Aunt Becky you saw on the show. She was a calm female presence amid the wacky, frat-boy antics of the guys. She knew how to laugh and have a good time, but she also knew when it was time to work. That was a good quality to have on our set. She was also a great friend and female mentor to us kids on the show. To this day, I love Lori to pieces. She is always genuinely interested in hearing about my life. She not only truly *listens*, but she remembers details and will ask me about them months later. That's a rare quality to find in *anyone* these days, much less in Hollywood. She is truly a class act—something I believe strongly, no matter what the headlines read on any given day. She is family.

Bob Saget was the most dad-like figure on the set, probably because he was a father to three daughters in real life as well. I think it was hard for outsiders to reconcile the fatherly Bob of *Full House* with the raunchy Bob of his stand-up comedy, but it's really not that hard for those of us who know him. It's simply different facets of his personality. He could easily go from fatherly concern about the kids on the set one minute to silly frat-boy jokes the next once he got around Dave and John. He is also a really fast talker: "How are you? Are you okay? How's your mom? What are you doing for dinner?" all in one single breath. He doesn't have time to wait for breaths . . . or even necessarily *answers*, for that matter! But I always felt loved and cared for by Bob nonetheless. His mind works a mile a minute, and we're all just here to try and keep up. I also don't think enough people know that he has the biggest heart of anyone I've ever met. He cares *so much* about the people around him, and he lets them know it. To know Bob is to be loved by Bob. His involvement with the Scleroderma Research Foundation in honor of his late sister Gay is evidence that his heart is as big as his personality. Underneath all the jokes and silliness lies a man who cares deeply and loves fiercely.

I remember one occasion that perfectly sums up Bob as the sentimental comedian. After going out for lunch on a break from shooting, we were driving back to the studio and Bob wanted to take a quick detour to visit Gay's grave. We all stood a few feet away to give Bob some space as he knelt at the headstone, completely silent. He traced Gay's name on the headstone with his fingers. After a few moments, he turned to us and said, "My parents wanted to name her 'Homosexual' but it wouldn't fit on the birth certificate." Oh, Bob! He has always used humor to cope with difficult or grief-filled moments. It's one of the things I love most about him.

His humor was once again appreciated one stressful week on set after John had been receiving death threats. It naturally put everyone on edge the entire week. The night of the audience show was particularly nerve-racking, with two hundred fans going through metal detectors (which was uncommon at the time) before sitting in the audience seats. During introductions, John paused before making his entrance and made the sign of the cross on his chest. Bob leaned over to him at that very moment to say, "John, can I have your parking space?" It was so untimely and so funny, and *so Bob*, that we all burst out laughing. We went on to have a great—and, thankfully, uneventful—show that night.

Even more than Bob, Dave Coulier was the cast member we could rely on the most to crack a joke at inopportune times. He was also the cast member we could rely on to crack a fart at pretty much any moment. Occasionally, he would entertain the audience with what our stage manager called "Celebrity Farts." There was a distinctive sound for each famous person, from John Goodman to Nancy Reagan. Part of it was his particular brand of funny, and I think part of it was just his propensity for flatulence! He would use a fart to punctuate a joke or sentence. He would use a fart to break the tension when things on set were dragging on too long or the director couldn't get his shot right. He would fart onstage, he would fart backstage. He would fart in front of anyone, any age, any role, any level of prestige on the set. Really, he was an equal fart opportunist. The worst was when he would wait until several of us castmates were gathered in the small space at the top of the kitchen stairs (an off-camera space that could only fit a handful of people at one time), and then let one rip as loudly as he could. We were trapped—literally trapped!—until our cue to enter the scene.

Dave would always feign innocence ("What did I do?") but we knew he secretly loved watching us recoil in horror at his odiferous habits.

Scott Weinger, who played D.J.'s boyfriend Steve in just over three seasons, was always the brainy one in the group. He left the show during the eighth and final season to attend Harvard University. He had already deferred one year to do the seventh season and couldn't defer again. I hired the same SAT tutor as him my senior year of high school. (I, however, did *not* get into Harvard.) Luckily for us, and the audience, he returned to do the final episode to take D.J. to prom. This was a surprise not only to D.J., but to Candace as well! People had been making guesses all week about who the "special guest" would be. Most people guessed Joey Lawrence. To everyone's delight, D.J. and Steve were reunited one last time.

Scott is one of the smartest people you will ever meet. He routinely regales us with obscure but highly accurate facts, and he reads books like biographies about Thoreau for fun. I secretly wonder if he writes encyclopedias in his spare time. But not only is Scott one of the smartest people you will ever meet, he is also one of the happiest. Boundless energy! Never have I seen this guy in even the slightest bad mood. The worst I've seen was in Tokyo, when he completely panicked because we couldn't find his favorite sushi bar. He trekked half the cast through the streets and subways of Tokyo trying to find this obscure joint. At last, we happened upon it (it's called Daiwa Sushi, in case you need a recommendation), and all eight of us crammed into the traditional sushi bar, where the sushi chefs yell at you as you enter and you don't order off the menu—you just eat whatever the chef puts in front of you. Scott ate there at least three more times during our stay in Tokyo. Even on our last day in Japan, he was texting everyone, "Sushi for breakfast? Anyone?" I swear, that guy could eat sushi for every meal of the day.

Although the entire cast was close, I was naturally closest with Candace Cameron and Jodie Sweetin simply because we were so similar in age. We shared a studio teacher for several years—as well as a classroom—which meant we had "school" together for three hours every day on our soundstage. (California law dictates that child actors must attend three hours of schooling every day with a licensed studio teacher. That packs in a lot of schooling, because you don't have roll call, recess, school announcements, or assemblies. It's nothing but concentrated study.) We all could relate to the pressures of balancing school with a full-time professional acting job. I think child actors in general are smart and self-driven—they have to be—so the schoolwork and tests weren't too difficult. The challenge was the juggling act of finding three hours each day where we could squeeze in and prioritize school. Rehearsal days were easier because we would have school for three straight hours in the morning while our stand-ins (people who would literally "stand in" and read our lines) took notes for us during scene rehearsals. But tape days were a little trickier because that's when the cameras were rolling, and we physically needed to be there. Oftentimes, we had to "bank" school hours, which meant doing extra school beyond the three hours on days when we had lighter schedules. Basically, child actors are always "working," be it at school or rehearsal or taping, all the time. There wasn't much time to turn off our brains and just chill.

It wasn't all hard work, though. Our studio teachers planned fun field trips for us, too, like the time we took the train down to the San Diego Zoo. That was our "school" for the day! When I was taking Spanish in high school, my studio teacher, Elise, brought me to Olvera Street, a historic district in downtown Los Angeles filled with restaurants, shops, and boutiques, paying homage to Old Mexico. Elise's rule was that I could speak only in Spanish—no English whatsoever. We had lunch and spoke Spanish to the servers and each other. It was great, real-world practice to go hours without being able to communicate in English.

There were several years when I was closer to Jodie than any of the other cast members. She's five years younger than I am—which is a lifetime when you're eight and thirteen. (We don't notice our age difference now—ha!) But we loved hanging out together. I had always felt a little more immature, socially, and underdeveloped for my age, so maybe hanging out with someone five years younger was more relatable to me. At the time, Candace just seemed older. She was too cool for the New Kids on the Block pillowcases that decorated my room. Candace's sister, Bridgette, was really into NKOTB like me, and she was also a stand-in on the show. I was going to marry Joe and she was going to marry Jon, so, as future sisters-in-law of sorts, we had a lot in common.

Jodie and I loved going to the mall and shopping together with our moms. One of our favorite activities was to go to Disneyland together using our annual passes. Nothing was better than riding the Matterhorn on a rainy day when hardly any other patrons were in the park, or sitting together on the curb to watch the Main Street Electrical Parade.

When *Full House* went on location to Hawaii, Jodie and I spent a lot of time together on our free days. One night, we discovered a dead frog that had been flattened by a car on the road outside our hotel. For some morbid reason, we decided to imitate this frog by posing our arms and legs in the same position as his flat little corpse. We thought we were hilarious, giggling hysterically as only little girls can do. We nicknamed the frog "Slim" and choreographed a little dance in his honor. What goofs we were!

If you are a hard-core fan of *Full House*, you may be thinking to yourself, "Wait. Kimmy Gibbler wasn't in the Hawaii episode . . ." And you would be correct! So why was I there? Because Kimmy *was* originally part of the script, until the very last minute. The night before we were scheduled to fly to Oahu, the producers called my parents and explained that my character had to be cut from the storyline because the script was too long. Heartbreaking, right? Except that our producers, some of the kindest people in Hollywood, told me I should come anyway. The flights and hotel were already booked and paid for, so my mom and I got to enjoy a week in Hawaii, and I got to swim and lay by the pool while the rest of the cast and crew worked. How lucky was I?

Many childhood friends experience childhood "firsts" together, and Candace, Jodie, and I were no exception. One of those "firsts" was a first kiss . . . and on television, no less. Candace and I both had our first kisses (in real life and on camera) on the same day during the "13 Candles" episode. I was thirteen in real life as well. It was D.J.'s thirteenth birthday in the episode, and her party included several rounds of the "Spin the Bottle" game. You know what that meant for us!

We were nervous. It was awkward. We asked Lori for advice. *How do you turn your head? Tongue or no tongue? Can you avoid the tongue? How fast can this be over?* First kisses are rarely perfect moments in real life, but having your first kiss EVER in front of a studio audience *and* your parents? Mortifying.

Somehow, we all survived to tell about it. And in one of the greatest throwbacks, we were able to use that footage of our first kisses from thirty years ago in a current episode of *Fuller House* when Kimmy's daughter, Ramona, played by Soni Bringas, has *her* first kiss. ("Ramona's Not-So-Epic First Kiss," season two.) And, you guessed it, that episode was Soni's first-ever kiss too, both in real life and on camera. Talk about a full circle moment.

Being the "offbeat" character means I had a lot of "offbeat" boyfriends in the show. There were no bona fide heartthrobs for Kimmy Gibbler. This means I had to kiss a few boys that I really didn't want to kiss. I won't name names (gosh, I hope none of them are reading this!), but there was one actor in particular . . . I was just NOT feeling it. We didn't get along super well, and being around him made me feel rather uncomfortable. Annnnd, of course, I had to make out with him in several scenes. Our producers knew I was hating this and wanted to make sure I was comfortable moving forward. They told me I didn't have to kiss him for real in rehearsals, that I could wait until the cameras were rolling if that would put me more at ease, which it did. Lori, again to the rescue, pulled the kid aside and told him in her no-nonsense manner, "No tongue!"

I had everyone in my corner, which was great. But I still had to kiss the guy for several on-camera takes. I was a teenager— an insecure and inexperienced teenager—and the situation was beyond mortifying. After the last scene, I ran straight to my dressing room. On my desk was an enormous bag of Hershey's Kisses with a note from our producers attached: "Here are some kisses we KNOW you will enjoy. Thanks for being a great sport." I smiled out of relief and gratitude. I really did have the best family on the *Full House* stage.

Kimmy's high school boyfriend, Duane (played by Scott Menville), was my personal favorite love interest. His chilled-out, aloof character who only replied, "Whatever . . ." to any and every question was the perfect counterpart for Kimmy's talkative, outgoing personality. Scott was also just a really cool guy, and so easy to work with. My favorite episode with him is the one where Kimmy and Duane flee to Reno to have a shot-gun wedding. They choose a *Friday the 13th* theme for their wedding, so naturally Duane wears a blood-soaked white tuxedo and Kimmy wears a blood-soaked veil with a hatchet in her head. Every bride's dream wedding, right? The absurdity of this situation was just so fun and funny to perform, even if the wedding was stopped at the last minute by Jesse and Danny, who convince Kimmy that she's too young to get married.

Over the course of eight seasons, the show would rise to monumental success, but we had no idea it was developing such a cult-like following. Sure, the ratings told us we were successful. But remember, this was in the age before social media. Pre-Internet, too. So I didn't really *feel* the success aside from the ratings. That is, until we traveled to Disney World.

We had a seventh season location shoot at Disney World in Florida for an episode revolving around the family (plus Kimmy) vacation, and Michelle becoming the theme park's princess for a day. We had huge sections of the park roped off for our production, and we drew enormous crowds. Fans would follow us into the public restrooms and pass notes under the stalls to ask for our autographs. Thank God this was before the era of selfies. Nobody needs a selfie in a public bathroom! It was the first time I'd really felt just how big the show had become.

Candace, Jodie, and I (and sometimes Mary-Kate and Ashley, too) started booking Sail With The Stars cruises, which was a chartered boat ride with several stars of '90s shows (Jenna von Oy from *Blossom*, the Mowry sisters from *Sister, Sister*). Fans were able to sail with us for a four-day cruise and participate in fun activities like group line dancing, autograph sessions, etc. This was a ton of fun for us girls (I even celebrated my sixteenth birthday on one of these cruises). But it also brought home how popular the show had become. People were spending money to go on vacation with us! We had security on board! This was still quite a trip for me, the kid who grew up doing commercials but still had to do chores at home.

Those cruises were also special, because that's where I met my real-life high school boyfriend, Ben. Ben was family friends with Jonathan Taylor Thomas (of *Home Improvement* fame) and had accompanied the family on one of the cruises. He was easily the most handsome boy I had ever laid eyes on, and I fell for him immediately. I kinda couldn't believe that he was interested in me, as I still saw myself as the gangly, awkward one. But I was drunk in love. We promised to stay together after the cruise even though he lived on the east coast and I lived on the west coast. He flew out for my winter formal dance that year, even though it was a tape night for me and I had to get special permission to leave the set early. Once again, the producers proved that they cared most about the people over the production. They arranged to tape all of my scenes first so I could make it in time for my dance. Ben came to the set and changed into his tuxedo in the schoolroom, where my dad helped him with his tie. He looked so handsome. Our hair and makeup artists did special makeup and an updo for me. Ben and I took pictures in front of the fake fireplace in the living room set. And then we took a picture with the *entire* cast in front of the audience. If Ben was embarrassed by all of this unusual attention, he didn't show it. He was a true gentleman. After the cameras finished snapping, we were whisked away in a private car to my winter formal, where we danced all night with all of my high school friends. It remains one of my favorite childhood memories.

Full House was rising in popularity at a rapid speed, but on Stage 24 in Burbank, things felt smaller within our tight-knit little family. Every Friday night before our 5:00 P.M. audience show, Bob would organize where the cast would go for dinner. We didn't *have* to go anywhere; the show provided a catered dinner or meal vouchers for the Warner Bros. commissary for cast and crew every Friday. But it was a bonding experience for the cast. It was just for us, not for the crew, someone's agent, or any significant others. The only loophole was for kids— sometimes Bob's daughters would join us at the dinners. Kids are always welcome at any *Full House* family gathering.

Mostly, the dinners were a way to get off the lot, to clear our minds and just laugh together for an hour before we buckled down for the live show. These dinners, often at Jerry's Deli, other times at one of the numerous restaurants at nearby City-Walk, are some of my fondest memories of my days on *Full House*. Funny side note: At one of these dinners, a fan came up to Bob and asked if we were the actors from *Full House*. "No," Bob said. "But we are their stand-ins." The best part (or maybe the worst) is that *the fan believed him*. She said okay and walked away! I just shook my head. To know Bob is to understand and accept his quirky kind of humor.

Another favorite fan moment occurred in the parking garage at CityWalk. Bob and I were standing together, waiting for the valet to bring around his car. A fan came up to me and nervously asked, "Are you Kimmy Gibbler from *Full House*?" I said yes, and she shared her excitement about the show with me before walking away. Without skipping a beat, I turned to Bob and said, "She didn't recognize *you*!" Instead of being offended, Bob grinned really, really big. I think he was legitimately proud of me for making this joke.

I'd be remiss if I didn't mention Mary-Kate and Ashley Olsen. Reporters love to ask us current cast members, "Will the Olsens ever come back? Why won't they come back?" To be honest, this question gets a little tiresome, if for no other reason than that it's already been asked and answered . . . repeatedly! But those inquiring minds keep inquiring, I guess. Mary-Kate and Ashley were a cornerstone of the original *Full House* series, and Jeff Franklin really wanted them to come back for the new series. I think that fans did, too, because there was so much curiosity: What is Michelle like now? But when it came time to start shooting *Fuller House*, the Olsens decided they didn't want to be on television anymore. They have found major success in the fashion industry and moved on to different passions. That's why the writers and showrunners set it up in that first episode that Michelle has a career in fashion now and lives in New York City (a nod to the Olsens' real-life career path). I can certainly relate to the feeling of finding other passions outside of Hollywood—more on that later—and I applaud them for sticking to what their hearts told them to do instead of caving to public pressure. We chose different directions. We all respect each other's decisions, and we are very happy for them. It's really that simple of an answer.

Back when we were costars, I wasn't really close with Mary-Kate and Ashley, simply because of our age difference. They were just nine months old when they started on the show, so most of what I remember is them learning to become child actors. As they got older, they were pretty good at staying on their mark (though they did ask "why?" an awful lot, as toddlers are wont to do). And speaking of toddler behaviors, the one funny thing I remember from those early days was what they did when they just weren't in the mood to follow directions. I don't blame them at all; a TV set is a very unnatural environment for a small child—*any* small child, even ones who love the job. So when Mary-Kate and Ashley didn't want to say their lines or stay on their marks, they'd say "I'm going to sing." That was their version of a tantrum—to sing instead of following directions.

Now that we're all adults, I can see that the rest of the cast bonded in a way that didn't include the Olsens, simply because they were so much younger than the rest of us. Mary-Kate and Ashley were babies and toddlers for half the length of the series. The whole experience was very different for them as the youngest children on the set. Today, they have closer friendships with Bob and John, but I just don't think they bonded with the cast as a whole the way the rest of us did. And that is the long answer to that overly asked question. There is no salacious headline here, folks. You wanted the truth? You got it, dude.

I really do feel like I grew up with a second family on the *Full House* set, and not simply because we all spent so much time working together. We genuinely cared about each other (and still do!). We could work forty hours a week together and not even bat an eye about spending the weekend together, too, going swimming at John Stamos's house—something we did fairly often. The older I get, the more I realize just how special it is to have loved ones like my *Full House* family.

CHAPTER FOUR
A Normal(ish) Kid

DESPITE THE OVERWHELMING REACH of the show, I didn't think my life was so different from that of other kids. I went to my local public high school, which I attended full-time on all my days off. On working days, I went to at least first period before the drive to Hollywood. I went to my formals and proms. I went to football games on Friday nights . . . or at least the second half, after we were done taping *Full House*. My best friend wasn't an actor but a fellow fourteen-year-old girl who offered to let me borrow her colored pencils the first week of school for an art project—I'd missed most of the week due to work. Ellen is still my best friend to this day. I know people will be disappointed to learn that Candace and I, while extremely close, are not actual BFFs. (She and her real-life BFF, Dilini, also met when they were young teenagers.) But Ellen has blond hair, and she's loyal and accepting and forgiving when I forget to call her back. In that sense, she is a lot like my own personal D.J. Tanner.

It was almost like I was leading a teenage double life. I

would wake up and prepare my own breakfast, then do the dishes, make my bed, go to first-period Spanish, and then hightail it (well, as fast as you can hightail anything in L.A. traffic) out to Stage 24 at Warner Bros. for rehearsals. Next it was preshooting, hair and makeup, more school (but this time with my tutor), and a live audience show on Friday nights. I could be cheering for my high school's basketball team one day and shaking hands with Magic Johnson at a network party the next. My life was extraordinary and ordinary, all at the same time.

But it was my life, and it was all I'd ever known. I give any and all credit to my parents, who fought hard to make sure I lived a normal childhood. They negotiated with the producers so I could attend that first-period class each day. They had meeting after meeting with the principal and teachers at my school so I could do both public school and remote school with a tutor on set. My tutor, Elise, generously worked with my teachers to ensure that the school year ran smoothly. She asked what worked best for them to keep me on track. Daily reports? Weekly reports? Quarterly reports? Did they want *her* to grade the papers, or did they want to do that themselves?

My parents encouraged my friendships and activities outside of school and work. I earned $5 for washing my dad's car on the weekends and another $5 for washing my mom's. This was my spending money—and it was a lot at the time! Perhaps most importantly, they always made sure I knew that I could leave Hollywood the moment I decided I hated my job (barring any current contracts with TV networks, of course).

"You can quit acting anytime you want," they would tell

me. "You just can't quit in the middle of traffic on the 101 freeway when you're overtired and hungry." Fair enough.

So that's what I did. I auditioned *a lot*. I worked regularly. I
hung out in a tree in my neighbor's front yard. I wrote a lot. I
read a lot. I memorized scripts. I spent a lot of time sitting in
the back seat of my mom's car in traffic on the freeway. And
once, in middle school, during the four-month-long hiatus between seasons of *Full House*, I decided I didn't want to act
anymore. I wanted a break. I was tired of being on the freeway
all the time, and I wanted more time to be a kid.

My parents said, "Okay. Write a letter to Judy."

So I did just that: "Dear Judy, I'd like to take a break. I
don't want to go on any auditions for four months. Kay?
Thanks, bye!"

Actually, I don't remember exactly what I wrote. But it was
something like that. And Judy, bless her heart, was one of
those rare Hollywood agents who cared more about her kids
(clients) than she did about the bottom line. In the same vein as
my parents, she understood, never tried to convince me otherwise, and encouraged me to "just be a kid."

Four months later, I was back—refreshed, renewed, and
ready to work again. Not long after that, I became a full-time
cast member on *Full House*, appearing in all episodes for the
duration of the series.

I don't remember the first time I got recognized in public. I
guess I was too young and oblivious to notice. My mom tells
me that when we used to eat out at a restaurant as a family,
people would whisper and stare but never approach.

As I got older, and as *Full House* became more popular, the whispers and stares began to multiply. One scenario that transpired more times than I could count: I would detect people in a group whispering and staring and trying to determine, "Is that . . . ?" Finally, the group would nominate a brave representative to come over and ask me. When I would tell the brave soul, "Yes, I'm *her*," they would whoop and holler and run back to the group: "It IS her!" I chuckle that no one, not even the representative, wanted to talk to me further. The just wanted a confirmation, I guess!

As I became an adult and had kids of my own, my looks changed and I aged, of course, but I have never not been recognized. It has always been a constant in my life. Sure, it slowed down a lot in those in-between years. But it's never been completely absent from my life. It's just the things people say to me that changed. Kids would ask me how old I am, and then would be shocked to learn that I'm old enough to have kids of my own. "But on TV . . ." Yes. On TV, I'm a teenager. Funny how kids have always had trouble with the concept of the passage of time and reruns on TV.

There was a significant chunk of my life when people would recognize me, but they couldn't place from where. "Do we go to church together? Do our kids play soccer together? Where do you work? Where have I seen you before?" Depending on my mood, I would:

1. Let them search for a bit before telling them.
2. Tell them who I was right away (if I was in a hurry).
3. Just let them hang! Sometimes I just didn't feel like talking about it.

With the birth of *Fuller House*, my fame has morphed once again. "Where do I know you from?" has shifted to "You're Andrea Barber! From *Fuller House*! Kimmy Gibbler!" Vague, confused recognition has given way to people now knowing my first and last name *and* that of my favorite band.

As a result of this lifetime evolution of fame, I have developed a sixth sense when it comes to being recognized. (I'm certain most celebrities have this sixth sense.) I can walk into a room and instantly feel if there are fans present. I can tell just by looking at someone if they watch my show. And I can almost always guess whether or not that person will be brave enough to ask me about it. Sometimes, when I see someone struggling with it, I'll just jump to the chase, "Yep! That's me! I'm *that girl* from *that show*."

Most of the time I don't mind being recognized at all; I love interacting with fans. I like finding out what we have in common. What I enjoy the most is when fans stop treating me like a celebrity and we can drop the pretenses and just hang like pals. I once put out an alert on Twitter that I was looking for a ticket to NKOTB's town hall meeting in April of 2012—sort of like an informal Q&A hosted by the band.

Anyone who knows me knows that I am a *huge* Blockhead, a.k.a. a lifelong devoted fan of the '80s band New Kids on the Block. I've loved them since I was thirteen years old, and the fandom has only grown since the band's reunion in 2008. The Blockhead community is a large, strong one. The New Kids even wrote a song called "Five Brothers and a Million Sisters" to describe the family-like bond Blockheads have made with each other over the years.

But back to the Town Hall. So I heard the New Kids were coming to Santa Monica, and I had no tickets to this event. (This was before I became friends with the band members—be still, my heart!) So I casually tweeted, "Anyone have a 'plus one' they'd be willing to share with me?"

In hindsight, that sounds like a stupid question, but remember—this took place before the resurgence of *Fuller House*. Plus, I have that bad habit of forgetting that a lot of people consider me a celebrity.

Cue a hundred replies to my Twitter request. Whoops! Fortunately, I'd gotten to know several Blockheads via Twitter, and they vouched for one fan in particular, whose name is, coincidentally, also Andrea.

Andrea said she would be happy to offer me her plus one, and her travel buddy, Lindsey, happened to have another plus one for *my* friend, Julie.

I said, "Great! Do you want to meet for a burger before the show?"

And so that is how one of my best friendships started. Andrea is a lifelong fan of both NKOTB and (coincidentally) *Full House*. We had burgers. We squealed over NKOTB. She never once mentioned *Full House*. My celebrity hat was off for the night, and we simply bonded over all things Joe and Jordan.

My point in telling this story?

I love my fans. I love that we have common interests. They love discovering that we both swoon over the same boy band. Is that weird? I'm not sure. But that doesn't matter to me.

But reconciling my fame and my normal personhood wasn't always so easy. When I was in high school, many kids would passive-aggressively let me know that they recognized me by mocking my character just within earshot: "Oooooh, Kimmy Giiiiiiibler! Don't take off your shooooooes!" *Funny, guys. Never heard that one before.* Kids in high school are simply immature and mean. To anyone. It doesn't really matter who you are; kids will home in on the one thing that makes you different and make fun of it. Red hair, too tall, too skinny, too round, too many freckles, big hair—you name it, kids will make fun of it. And the thing that made me stand out was the fact that I was on TV. So the mean kids would ridicule me for it, write stupid things on my locker, and "gleek" at me. Gleeking, one of the dumber high school antics, is when you build up saliva in your mouth and then shoot it out between your teeth, usually at an impressive distance. I distinctly remember walking down a set of stairs and feeling wet remnants of kids gleeking at me. Gross, right? Welcome to high school.

None of this was pleasant, and I have no doubt it was highly upsetting to me at times. But what I remember most was feeling thankful that I had a solid set of friends who I could count on to not be jerks. I was never part of the popular crowd, but I also never felt a longing to be popular, either. I just wanted to be part of a group that was *kind*. And I found them. We weren't into gossip or popularity contests. We were into Taco Bell and another hit show at the time, *Beverly Hills, 90210*. We were into Yearbook and Spirit Week and cheering for the basketball team. These friends, and particularly my best friend, Ellen, were what made high school memorable.

Between my high school friends, my real family who kept me grounded, and my second TV family whom I adored, I had a very solid upbringing that was free of drama and scandals. I had zero desire to go to Hollywood parties, zero desire to try drugs or alcohol. I felt fulfilled by my life and didn't have any need to push the boundaries. Sorry to be so boring, but not all child stars end up as scandalous headlines, and those (few) who do are featured prominently to line the pockets of those publishing the headlines. The media loves nothing more than a public breakdown.

As I got older, my parents continued to be my best advocates, and I think this was the most critical element in raising a "normal" child and teenage actor. I was required to do chores. I always had to keep my room tidy. I was home for dinner most nights. I was not allowed to go to many industry parties, which was fine with me because why would I want to drive all the way out to Hollywood to make small talk with strangers when all of my friends were at the basketball game in my high school gym?

My parents kept all of my earnings in a trust fund that I wasn't allowed to touch until I turned eighteen years old. (The first thing I "bought" was my tuition for my freshman year at Whittier College, followed by my first car, an Acura Integra.) My parents never did tell me how much money I was earning per episode. Why? Because a very common question I was asked was, "How much money do you make on TV?" And my parents figured if I didn't know, I could legitimately tell people, "I don't know," instead of being placed in a really awkward position as a teenager being asked a rather intrusive question. It was a blessing, I now realize.

Not focusing on money also enabled me to feel like this whole acting thing was a hobby instead of a career, which I think is a really healthy attitude for child actors to have. It wasn't my livelihood, I wasn't being forced to do it, and I could stop whenever it wasn't fun anymore.

My parents read each script for every potential job and turned down the ones they felt were inappropriate. One movie script required that the eleven-year-old girl take off her shirt and run into the ocean. It was probably written to be harmless, but for their eleven-year-old daughter, it just didn't feel right. So Mom and Dad turned it down.

My parents also expected me to go to college. In fact, my dad, acting as my attorney, negotiated a "college clause" in my contract which stipulated that I could leave the *Full House* series *at any time* if I decided I wanted to pursue college full-time and/or out of state. I never needed to execute that clause; the series ended during my freshman year of college (which I decided to attend part-time so I could still do the show). But it was valuable to have that option because—and I can't stress this enough—you can't rely on just your acting skills to get through life. You need to have something else to fall back on. Most actors are either unemployed and waiting tables, or acting . . . but usually not enough to make a living. According to some statistics, only 15 percent of Screen Actors Guild members earn enough to qualify for health insurance from acting wages alone.

Parents come up to me all the time and ask, "I want to get my kid into acting. Do you have any advice?" Yes, I have advice. But more importantly, I have questions! Why are you doing this? Do you know how much work it is for both the child *and* the parent? You say your child is gifted? And Hollywood is her calling? Put her in a play! What's wrong with local theater?

Perhaps I side-eye too many people and don't give them enough credit. But I question why people would ever want to put their child in a business where there are so many potential pitfalls. If child actors get such a bad rap, why do you want your child to be one?

Don't get me wrong: I'm really not that negative about child actors in Hollywood. I had an exceptionally positive experience as a child actor. But I'm being realistic when I acknowledge that it is a tough business that requires children to adapt to an adult world at a very young age. We require them to sit still for very long periods of time, we separate them from (most) other children for eight hours a day, and we demand they follow specific directions, like, "Finish speaking by the time you land on this precise mark," or "Wait for the laughs." It's a very unnatural environment for small children. We ask *a lot* of them, and I can see when that wiggly, overtired kid just wants to run outside with other kids.

The basic needs of childhood have nothing to do with the entertainment industry. Hopefully this goes without saying, but it's critical that parents look out for their child's best interest—not fame, not fortune, not attention, but *what are your child's needs at this specific time in their lives?* It seems like a no-brainer, but there is a reason why social workers are required on set any time children are working. The director can't get the shot he needs and wants to work the children late into the night? Nope! There's a law protecting them. Mom and Dad want to spend little Jimmy's hard-earned money on a new beach condo for themselves? Nope! Enter the Coogan Law, which protects the child's right to a trust fund. Kids need advocates, and the most important people they need in their corner are their parents.

I feel extraordinarily lucky that I didn't have to grow up in the age of explosive social media attention. I can't fathom how difficult it would be to grow up exposed in the fishbowl of the Internet, with people watching every move you make and retweeting everything you say. It's weird enough trying to navigate this new digital landscape as an adult.

When I was growing up, there was no Twitter, no Instagram, no red carpets, no cultivating your "brand." (That word makes me cringe.) It was pretty much exclusively about the work. You work hard, you continue to work! Brand, image, glam— none of that existed in my world. Somewhere along the way, the culture shifted, and being a "celebrity" became almost more important than talent. I'm not so sure I would want to be a child actor in today's celebrity-obsessed culture. That golden era of "just being a kid" on a sitcom seems like a long, long time ago. I'm grateful, now more than ever, for the positive experience I had as a child actor.

CHAPTER FIVE

My Hollywood Exit

IT STRIKES ME AS ODD when people ask, "Why did you leave acting?" because I never really made the conscious decision to leave, nor did I make any dramatic proclamations. "I'm leaving . . . and I'm never coming back!" [*Slams door.*] I just never made a deliberate decision to return—until I had a reason and a desire.

ABC announced that *Full House* would be ending its eight-year run three weeks before we were scheduled to shoot the season eight finale. It was a surprise announcement, and we were all a bit shell-shocked, especially considering that the series was one of ABC's most popular shows, having led off the well-known TGIF lineup on Friday nights for many years. With just three weeks before we took our final bow, our writers felt unprepared to write a proper series finale, and we as actors felt unprepared to say goodbye to our beloved show.

The final episode turned out to be a bit of an unusual one, with Michelle falling off a horse and developing amnesia before she finally remembers her family again, but it was our best try at a finale on such short notice. With hot tears stinging our eyes and giant lumps in our throats, we took our final bows at curtain call. It was definitely a loss for us and for the fans.

Despite the sadness at the series' abrupt ending, *Full House* wrapped its eight-year run at an ideal time for me. I was in my first year of college, and I had new and exciting prospects on the horizon. I was transitioning from child to adult, moving out of my childhood bedroom and into the dorms. College is a time to discover new things about yourself and explore all kinds of subjects. I discovered that I hate science and love the arts. I discovered that I hate cigarettes. And I discovered that I love, love, *love* travel. My semester abroad in Copenhagen, Denmark, during my junior year was so life-altering that I worked in study-abroad programs as my first career post-college. I felt fulfilled in ways that I never had before.

I think that this is part of why I never felt a lasting void in my life after *Full House*; my life as a college student filled that void. Of course, I was sad when *Full House* ended. We all cried during our last curtain call. I was going to miss seeing all of these wonderful, dear people in my life every day. That is what I was saddest about: missing the *people,* not the profession. Being an actor was fun, but it was the friends who took up residence in my heart. I wonder if, on some level, I knew (hoped?) that we would all stay in touch over the years, which made the whole thing a little less sad for me.

I truly believe that college is a glorious period for growing self-awareness. I couldn't wait to move into my dorm room. I was so ready for independence. College was a thousand times better than high school, because I felt in charge of my own life for the first time. I could pick my own schedule and the subjects I wanted to study. I lived on my own (well, the dorm was the closest thing to living "on my own" I had ever experienced up to that time). My roommate freshman year was a quiet girl who wore a prosthetic leg. I only mention this because I feel like it was a big thing we had in common: There was something different about both of us that made us stand out and could possibly make us self-conscious because students were probably talking about it behind our backs. People would ask her, "Are you roommates with the girl from *Full House*?" Similarly, they would ask me, "Are you roommates with the girl with the fake leg?" But in reality, these things that made us different were not a big deal to us. They were just one part of who we were. We didn't talk much, but when we did, she never once asked me about the show. And I never really talked about her leg unless she needed help retrieving it from across the room. It was actually a great pairing because we were both able to be pretty nonchalant about our differences.

Besides the occasional whispers throughout the campus, I felt like I was studying alongside real, mature people for once. High school had been so full of irritating jerks who just loved poking fun at me, writing rude things on my locker, snickering behind my back, and yelling "Gibbler!" as I walked by them. My college peers, by contrast, were unfazed by my celebrity past, or at least respectful about it. That immature teasing was no longer part of my day-to-day life. Fellow students would recognize me in passing, but it wasn't anything more than a blip on their radar. I guess everyone had moved on.

Or maybe I had moved on, I don't know. By the end of freshman year, the question about my former life was more like part of a survey: "What's your name? What dorm do you live in? Were you that girl on *Full House*? What's your major?" I became really good at blending in, which is what I wanted most. Other students might ask a question or two about *Full House*, but then the topic of conversation would quickly move on to more important things, like who was pledging which sorority or what was that mystery meat in the cafeteria.

Speaking of sororities, I did end up pledging—twice, in fact. Whittier College doesn't take part in the Greek letter organizations, so technically we called our fraternities and sororities by the catch-all term "Societies." But they were very similar in nature to traditional fraternities and sororities. The first society I picked was the most popular girls' society, and they really wanted me to pledge. I felt so desired. And by the popular crowd! This was unfamiliar territory for me, because despite being on a hit TV show for the majority of my teen years, I had never been the popular kid in high school. So this was exciting stuff.

The pledging period, however, felt tedious. It was never like "hazing" or anything dangerous, per se. I just didn't understand the point of it all. The girls who had previously befriended me to get me to pledge their group were now suddenly cold and mean. We had an extensive list of day-to-day tasks we had to do that took up every ounce of free time we had. I never understood the point of those daily tasks. Meanwhile, I was supposed to be bonding with these virtual strangers and referring to them as "sisters." All of it felt so forced. Every day, I had the growing feeling that I wasn't in the right place. Nothing sat right with me. So, after a week, I left (or "depledged," as they called it). I'm sure this wasn't the cool thing to do, and I imagine it wasn't well received by the girls in the society. But I just wasn't willing to put up with any of it anymore. And those girls never really spoke to me again, except occasionally in passing.

Meanwhile, I was developing friendships with other girls, many of whom were part of a different female society called the "Palmers." This wasn't necessarily the coolest or most popular group; girls weren't clamoring to try to get a bid to pledge. This group was just down to earth. They were real. Most importantly, I had already started developing genuine friendships with many of these gals. They were my friends before pledging. They were still my friends when I declined their (first) bid to pledge. They were my friends when I was pledging another society. They were my friends after I depledged that group. I felt like their friendship wasn't conditional on my picking their group. So I picked them to pledge the following year, and it felt like I was finally where I was supposed to be.

The pledging period was still hard, but it felt meaningful the second time around. That period was about performing tasks that related to learning about the history and traditions of the Palmer Society, traditions that spanned over seventy-five years. Our activities really made me feel bonded to the group. We explored the meaning behind the symbols of our diamond-shaped crest and lavalier; learned about Alice Freeman Palmer (for whom the group is named), a prolific advocate of higher education for women during the nineteenth century; and memorized traditional songs that had been sung by generations of

Palmers who came before us. It felt, genuinely, like a sister-hood. Those girls are still some of my best friends to this day. And I still wear my Palmer sweatshirt to bed many nights.

I majored in English literature and found so much fulfill-ment in my English courses. My brain was like a sponge; it couldn't soak up enough books, ideas, theories, and analyses. I devoured the works of Henry David Thoreau and Walt Whit-man and their writings on nature and finding peace. Learning about deconstructionism—what makes a text whole and the holes in between; taking apart what's said and what's left un-said—was a mind-blowing experience during my senior year. It was the first time I had viewed a text, or *the world*, really, as something to be interpreted, not simply read or observed. Up until then, I read texts the way I thought I was supposed to. De-constructionism taught me that there is no right or wrong way of looking at things; it's how you interpret a text that gives it meaning.

I also really enjoyed my writing classes and excelled in them. In one of those early classes, the professor made copies of my paper to hold up as an example to the rest of the class. Whoa!

"Now this is how you were *supposed* to do the assignment," she lectured to the class. I was flattered, but also flabbergasted. Really? *My* paper? I didn't even feel like it was my strongest piece of work; I just took my thoughts from my brain and pushed them out onto the page, like stream of consciousness.

I think I did so well with writing because that's where I felt most comfortable. It was a heck of a lot easier than having to *say* what I was thinking out loud. Class participation was—

well, let's just say that wasn't my strongest area by a long shot. This may sound odd, but speaking up in class was totally different than performing on a soundstage. I remained silent through most classes, even the smaller ones with a twelve-student maximum. When the professor would do an exercise that involved going around the room to solicit answers or ideas, I would usually freeze up.

"Andrea? Do you have anything to add?" Dr. Adams, my professor of English literature, would ask.

"Ummm. Well . . . um, I agree with everyone else," I would finally manage.

It's not that I didn't have ideas or answers. I had lots of things to say! But this is a common occurrence in my Anxious Brain: My mind starts spinning, and then I start overthinking, and then I'm afraid I'll mess up, and . . . and . . . my mouth just can't make sense of it all.

I stay paralyzed in this space. And so I stay quiet.

The same holds true today, even though I'm a lot older and more experienced, and I've faced a lot of my fears. People ask me why I'm so quiet in TV interviews. Well, because old habits are hard to break. My brain's automatic response is the "flight" option between "fight or flight." Sometimes, I can get a good handle on it and avoid the flight. Oftentimes, I don't. This is just how I'm wired. I accept it and do the best I can. It's all I can do.

You can probably see now why I prefer writing to pretty much *anything* else. It's easier to make sense of the noise in my brain when my words come out through my fingers. I can take a beat and think. I can edit if I mess up. I can express *exactly* what I mean when I write, not just fumble to get some random words out of my mouth when I'm asked a question on live television.

It's exhausting to read about this complicated process I put myself through during the simplest of tasks, isn't it? It's exhausting living it, too.

My junior year, as I mentioned, I decided to study abroad in Copenhagen, Denmark. This was Whittier College's flagship study-abroad program, and everyone highly recommended it. A group of my friends decided to sign up, so I had the courage to do the same. ("Friend influence" is a common theme throughout my life.) But I have to admit—everyone was right. It truly was the best decision I ever made.

To say I was nervous would be putting it mildly. Despite having had so many unique experiences as a child actor, I was actually a pretty sheltered kid. We never moved around when I was young; I grew up in the same bedroom in the same house for my entire childhood. And I didn't even go to college out of state—I was still very much within driving distance of my parents. Copenhagen was my chance to really explore a world outside of my own, both personally and as an American. But I was still seriously nervous.

I'd planned to live with a Danish host family, which was recommended to give a more immersive experience in the culture. I was assigned to live with a Danish mom and dad along with their three teenage children. Before I left the U.S., I had to write a letter to them describing myself. How on earth was I supposed to do that?

"Hello. I'm an awkward and anxious girl who is famous in

America, but I hope you don't think I'm a diva. Love, Andrea."
Do I even mention *Full House*? This was all very strange. I
ended up mentioning the show, because how awkward would
it have been had they seen the show and then suddenly Kimmy
Gibbler showed up at their door? But I also wrote that I didn't
like to make a big deal about that part of my life and was hoping to blend in in Denmark. Ha! The idea of *any* American student blending in anywhere *but* America is amusing to me now.
I stood out like a sore thumb. Not because I was a celebrity,
mind you, but because of my light wash, out-of-style jeans and
the massive, oversized parka I wore to endure the cold. There
was just no avoiding looking like an American.

My host family was truly wonderful. They mentioned the
show maybe once, but they were completely unfazed. They
treated me like any other American student they had hosted in
the past: They lightly teased me when my stupid American hair
dryer (even with the European converter) blew a fuse and left
the entire house without electricity. They convinced me that
taking twenty-minute hot showers was wasteful. They cooked
and coaxed me into eating wonderful, traditional Danish foods
that I couldn't pronounce, like *frikadeller* (meatballs) and *lev-
erpostej* (liver paste!) and *smørrebrød* (Danish open-faced
sandwiches). It was mostly delicious and, at times, a little
weird. My favorite treat was *æbleskiver*, Danish pancake balls
sprinkled with powdered sugar and served with jam. I loved
them so much, I bought an *æbleskiver* pan. To this day, I still
make them for my kids and bring them to potlucks at school.
They are a hit with the elementary school set.

They also taught me how to use public transportation, which

was a revelation for this Southern California girl who had always relied heavily on a car to get anywhere and everywhere. Public transport is the best invention ever. The trains were efficient and on time: If the train schedule had an arrival estimate of 11:02, it would be there at 11:02. They were clean, and no one talked to each other (my favorite part). Everyone read, so I studied on my daily forty-minute commute into the city for class.

My classes were part of the University of Copenhagen and taught by Danish professors, but it wasn't a fully integrated program; the classes were taught in English, and I was with exclusively American students. It was a program called "DIS," for Danish International Study, and it was on the smaller side, with about 250 students from colleges all around the U.S. (I was recognized more by my fellow Americans than I was by the Danes.) I took Danish ballet (history of ballet, not actual dancing), Danish politics and urban studies, and, my worst subject, Danish language. I had taken four years of Spanish in high school, but nothing prepared me for the mixing of vowels and strange consonants and deep, guttural pronunciations. I did my best and choked through my oral exams.

My time abroad was also punctuated by my first significant breakup. My boyfriend Jordan and I had been together for a year and a half, and we simply grew apart between the miles and life circumstances. During that first week of living in a foreign country, I felt the creeping depression that accompanies a breakup, compounded by the anxiety of being away from home. I didn't know where to turn. Fortunately, my friend and fellow study-abroad student Greg immediately recognized the panic on my face, hugged me, and promised he would help me through whatever struggle I was feeling. Some say you will meet your best friends in college, and this proved to be true with Greg. He was there for me yet again, so many years later, to help me heal during my divorce. Of the many gifts studying abroad gave me, I count Greg as one that I cherish the most.

The most invigorating thing about studying in a foreign country was waking up every day and knowing I was going to see or learn something completely new. My mind buzzed from so much different and challenging cultural and academic information. I loved exploring the city. I loved watching the seasons change and experiencing real *weather*—a novelty for a SoCal native. My mind opened for perhaps the first time to the idea that the way we do things in America isn't the only way. I learned about socialism and free health care, twelve-month paid maternity leave, and free higher education in Denmark. I also learned about high taxation. I also learned that kids in Denmark are given so many more responsibilities at a young age than American children. Toddlers there are given scissors in preschool, and they learn not to abuse them or cut themselves. I witnessed mothers leaving their babies in prams (strollers) outside the market so they could do their shopping without the pram taking up so much room. And the babies were completely safe! Nobody was ever harmed. The citizens aren't litigation-crazy. This is a country with very low crime rates, where trust thrives. Whether I agreed with socialism and this way of life was irrelevant; to *experience* it firsthand changed my perspective forever.

The program schedule included a two-week break in the

middle of the semester for travel. The first week, I took an organized study tour of Moscow and Saint Petersburg, Russia. I figured I might never get the chance to go to Russia ever again in my life, so I took the tour with other American students from DIS. We rode the night train (and survived) and went to see the Russian ballet. It was even more of a culture shock than being in Denmark. The food was so strange to me, and the entire country was very dark and cold that time of year (late October).

After my week in Russia, I had planned to go to Rome to meet up with Greg and other friends who hadn't gone on the Russia tour. I was the only one of this group of friends who went on the Russia trip, so it was up to me to get myself from Denmark to Italy, *all by myself*. Holy hell. I look back on it, and I wonder, "What was I *thinking?*" As a parent now, there is no way I would want my twenty-one-year-old daughter traveling alone from the very top of Europe to the very bottom. But, clearly, I survived it: two plane rides, a layover, and a train, all leading to the moment I spotted my friends in the Rome train station. This gave me a *massive* surge of confidence, and I really felt in that moment that I was invincible and could do anything. Little, sheltered Andrea, who rarely left Orange County—not even to go to college—just trekked across Europe by herself, navigated all these different methods of transportation completely solo, and lived to tell about it! I was on top of the world.

That's the thing about studying abroad. You learn more about *yourself* than the country you're visiting. You learn your capabilities and boundaries. You learn your tolerance. You learn that the only life you'd ever known is not the only way to live. You see the world through different eyes. That is the biggest souvenir of all. That knowledge, that perspective, that confidence . . . it all stays with you for the rest of your life.

So college fulfilled me in ways I hadn't ever been fulfilled before. I graduated with honors. And then I experienced what I imagine most recent college graduates experience immediately after the commencement high wears off: PANIC. *What the hell am I supposed to do now?*

My English literature degree didn't lay out a clear career trajectory, so I freaked. I thought maybe I would default to what I always did: acting. Did I even have any other skills? My insecurities suddenly ramped back up. I called my agent and asked if she would be willing to put me on the audition circuit again.

The minute I received my first post-college audition call was the minute I knew: There was not one ounce of me that wanted to get in my car and drive out to Hollywood. My heart just wasn't in it anymore. I still loved acting—the thrill of creating a character, memorizing lines, the feeling you get when you nail a joke, making people laugh. I loved the creative side of it. But the business . . . the business I never liked. Cattle-call auditions. Rejection, again and again. Knowing that it's not just talent, but looks and luck that can be the deciding factor in whether or not you book a job. The unpredictability of the schedule. Not knowing when you might be working again. And now, the branding of yourself.

I had changed too much to go back. I had found too many other passions. I was ready to create a different life. I felt very fulfilled by my fourteen-year acting career as a child. I had a lot of amazing experiences that many people only dream of. I couldn't ask for anything more.

"Don't cry because it's over," as they say. "Smile because it happened."

Without pursuing a career in acting or English literature, I did what any other bewildered graduate would do: took up an internship with the United Nations. That's random, right? I thought so, too, when one of my college professors, Dr. Mike McBride (affectionately known as "Doc"), approached me during my senior year and asked if I would be interested in a summer internship in Geneva, Switzerland, at the United Nations High Commissioner for Refugees (UNHCR). The thought of living abroad again made my heart swoon. But . . . the UN? Refugees? I subtly reminded Doc that I was an English major, not political science, though I had taken courses in both. Doc reassured me that I had what it takes to be a good intern in this position: writing skills.

"I can teach you everything else that you don't already know," he said. "But you already have the most important skill: you know how to write well. Which means you can do this internship."

Well, then! With an uncharacteristic leap of faith, I said yes. And then I promptly registered for as many political science and human rights courses that I could fit into my schedule. I also registered for Model United Nations, a simulation of the UN General Assembly where students learn about international relations and diplomacy.

Equipped with as much information as I could possibly hold in my brain, I moved to Geneva, Switzerland for four months and acted as an intern for UNHCR. I say "acted" because in many ways it felt like one big performance. I was acting like I knew what I was doing, but I was out of my element. I knew how to write, yes, but I had to work really hard to understand the issues and ethics at hand. I also had to work hard to grasp the language. And no, I don't mean a foreign language. I mean "UN speak." The United Nations uses words and acronyms— like CEDAW and ECOSOC—that are rarely used anywhere else in life. (Those stand for Convention on the Elimination of all Forms of Discrimination Against Women and Economic and Social Council, in case you were wondering!) I often had to refer back to my little cheat sheet to make sure I knew what everyone was talking about.

I also felt this weird detachment from what I was putting on paper. I was writing about the numerous challenges of internally displaced persons, or IDPs, which are actually much different challenges than those faced by refugees, an entirely different set of people. IDPs are displaced within the borders of their country, unlike refugees, who are outside the borders. And because IDPs can't seek asylum inside the borders of their own country, they face an even larger set of challenges. Yet the entire time I was writing about their struggles, I was working in this beautiful, modern building under maximum security, not to mention running water and air-conditioning. Who was I to be writing about the life-or-death struggles of IDPs and refugees in war-torn countries that I had only read about in my limited little life? I had compassion for these people and this subject, but was I even qualified to be writing about such struggles from my cushy high-rise?

Another part of my job was to attend the General Assembly meetings and take notes. The meetings were tedious. They could spend the better part of an hour debating the placement of a comma, no joke. It all felt extremely legal and formal. The meetings are moderated by a chair, and the countries have to be called upon before they can recite their pre-written speeches. I guess this is a very democratic, civilized way to run things, but just once I wanted to hear an impassioned debate between two countries' representatives!

My four months in Geneva gave me a very unique experience, and one that I'll never forget. But it was very different from my semester in Copenhagen. I didn't feel as culturally integrated, because Geneva is such an international, cosmopolitan city. The "culture" in Geneva was a combination of all the different citizens from around the world who gathered in the city to work at the United Nations. It didn't feel uniquely Swiss. I also didn't have a ton of friends there, because I worked mostly with older adults, except for one or two other American interns. So by the time my four months was up, I was ready to be home.

Back in California, I was offered a job that seemed right up my alley: Assistant Director of International Programs at Whittier College. That's a fancy title for someone who advises students and coordinates study-abroad opportunities for them. I was thrilled—I was in my comfort zone, I had experience living abroad, and best of all, I was (hopefully) helping students have life-changing experiences similar to the one I'd had in Copenhagen. It was a very fulfilling role for me.

I felt like I could really connect with the students, who were at all times curious, nervous, and excited. Only on a couple of occasions did a student stop by my office under the guise of wanting to know more about study abroad, then start asking questions about *Full House*. It didn't happen a lot, so I didn't mind. I would just reroute the conversation back to study abroad and, hey, maybe I inadvertently convinced a few students to go abroad who would have otherwise never inquired! But mostly, students had questions about where they should study abroad and whether their credits would transfer back to their college transcript. Everyone seemed to want to go to big cities: London, Sydney, Paris. My most common advice was to seek out programs in smaller cities and countries, like Ireland rather than England and New Zealand instead of Australia. I feel like students get a deeper cultural integration in smaller countries that aren't so tourist-driven. Plus, there is something about small countries that brings out a deep, national pride in its citizens.

My favorite part of my job was the debriefing sessions we would hold in the office a few weeks after the students returned from their semesters abroad. We would order pizza and go around the room, listening to students share their experiences out of the country. They were usually only gone four months, but the difference I saw between the nervous student I said "*au revoir*" to four months prior and the self-assured student in front of me at the debriefing was evident. I loved seeing that change, that air of confidence, the wide-eyed expression of having seen their world in a new way. It was the best. Decades later, while out to dinner, I actually had someone approach me, and the first thing he said was, "This is not what you think." Indeed, he didn't want an autograph or to talk about *Full House*. He wanted to tell me that I had helped arrange his study abroad and how meaningful that was. It was just as meaningful to me to get to hear what it meant to him so many years later.

I stayed with this job for a few years, and only left because I had a new goal on the horizon: getting my master's degree. Because I was so immersed in the world of international education, I learned that there were master's programs in England that only lasted twelve months. The idea of getting an advanced degree in as little as one year *and* living abroad again was tantalizing. So I applied and got accepted to University of York's Master's Programme in Women's Studies, which was a subject of passion for me. Once again, as with my English literature degree, I wasn't thinking practically about a field of study that would produce clear-cut job opportunities; I simply followed where my heart led me. (I was *very* privileged—I fully realize this.) And my heart led me to York, England.

I was newly married at the time—much more on this to come—and so my new husband Jeremy and I left three weeks after our wedding to go live in England for a year. Jeremy planned to study history at York, and I was enrolled in the oldest master's program in women's studies in all of the U.K. I was one of only two Americans in the entire program. *Gulp*.

Jeremy and I had our own little apartment in town and

would take the bus to university every day. We quickly grew accustomed to the tiny refrigerator in our flat and having to walk to get our groceries every other day. We made friends with a few British students at the university. They seemed *so much smarter* than we were. I'm not sure if it was just the accent or if they really were more intelligent. Probably a bit of both. But my intimidation quickly wore off, and we became good friends. We would frequently meet for coffee or tea or, if it was a weekend, a beer. One night, after I'd known our friends for at least six months, I had one too many beers and walked through the cobblestone streets of York, linking arms with our friends and shamelessly trying to imitate their English accents. At the time, I thought I was spot on! But then my friend Daniel told me (in the politest way possible) that my accent had actually transformed slowly from "English" to "Victorian Caricature," and lastly melding into what sounded most like an Irish peasant. Close enough, right?

And again, as in Copenhagen and Geneva and anywhere else that is not America, I was only recognized from *Full House* once or twice. About eight months into the program, I asked my British friends out of curiosity, "Did you know . . . ?" and they casually replied, "Yes, of course."

"But you never said anything?"

"No," our friend Gilly said. "We wanted to respect your privacy."

Maybe it was their courteous nature, or maybe it was the fact that *Full House* had been wrapped for almost ten years by this point. But to be considered and treated just like any other

normal person was such a relief. I wasn't given special attention, I wasn't treated like a celebrity. I was just *me*. And that
was a glorious feeling.

My M.A. program was small and challenging, and once
again my self-doubts led me to feel unqualified to be in the
same room as all of these really smart, international people. I
felt like the "dumb American" just trying to keep up. I don't
know why I never gained the confidence or believed in my capability to be there. But the classes were small (an average of
just fifteen students per class), so there was really no way to
hide my feelings of incompetence. I worried a lot about this.
So, of course, my anxiety—never fully leaving my body—
reared its ugly head again, and I had trouble sleeping. I tried
over-the-counter medications like Nyquil, and that helped, but
I was still wound pretty tight.

At this point in my life, I was fully aware that I felt anxious,
but I wouldn't know there was actually a name for what I
had—Generalized Anxiety Disorder—until much later in life.
That diagnosis came when I sought help for postpartum anxiety and depression (again, keep reading for much more on
that).

Other than my anxious self-doubts about my intellect, living
in England was a really incredible experience. It was an extraordinary way to spend my newlywed year with Jeremy: just
the two of us, no family obligations, learning the nuances of
British life together and traveling to new countries, with no real
distractions other than school. We loved exploring the U.K. by
train and watching miles and miles of uninterrupted, natural,
beautiful English countryside whiz by us. I loved experiencing

all types of weather within the same four-hour period: rain, sun, humidity, wind, and even the occasional hailstorm. I loved the convenient excuse of "being a foreigner" that somehow justified all the lame mistakes I made. (I wish I could maintain that excuse forever!) I loved how the English have respect for social rules and norms; watching those really long, straight queues of people form at bus stops was a fantastic sociological study. How respectful! And why can't Americans be this considerate of everyone around them? But mostly, I loved the same thing I'd always loved about living abroad: waking up every morning, knowing I would see or experience something new that day. We were very, very fortunate to experience that life for a year. I'll never take that for granted.

So that was my life post–*Full House* and pre-motherhood. Years later, when I returned for *Fuller House*, I frequently read online fan comments that said, "That Kimmy Gibbler girl did *nothing* after Full House!" As if I'd just been waiting around bored for twenty years until the *Fuller House* reunion was announced. Ha! I just smiled, knowing my twenty-year "break" was as full as it ever could be.

CHAPTER SIX

Marriage and Motherhood

I'LL BE FRANK AND SAY it's a little strange writing about the details of a marriage that has since been dissolved. Are my memories clouded by my feelings now, almost seven years since it ended? This sort of feels like writing a eulogy, except the other person is still very much alive and will probably be reading this. (Hi, Jeremy!) Maybe my memories are simply clouded because it's been seventeen years since I first got married, and my brain is old and dusty now.

Anyhow, I will do my best to write about this particular time period in my life in an honest and open way, while still respecting the privacy of my ex-husband and my kids. They deserve that. Jeremy and I still interact and co-parent together every day in a respectful and friendly way (though it wasn't always like this, as you'll see). And besides, I'm not one to throw shade in a public manner. I much prefer to throw shade under my breath to my closest friend where no one else can hear me. (Just sayin'!)

So where do I begin? I first met Jeremy when I was twenty-four, just a few years out of college. We were both out at a piano bar at the Irvine Spectrum—he was with his Marine friends, and I was with my college sorority girlfriends. I remember walking up to him and flirtingly scratching the back of his "high and tight" military haircut. This is how I flirted back then—by scratching a guy's head. Clearly, my game was strong.

He had no idea that I had been a celebrity. He actually didn't have a clue until our third or fourth date, when I left the table to go use the ladies' room and a fan approached him and asked, "Is your girlfriend on TV?" I came back from the restroom and he told me, laughing, "Those girls over there think you're on television. Isn't that ridiculous?" I broke the news to him that it wasn't actually so ridiculous. He didn't seem fazed by my recognizability, though, and show business hadn't been part of my life for many years by that point. So our relationship continued like any other normal couple's would.

We got engaged a year later and married a year after that. Planning my wedding was one of the first times I remember my anxiety reaching a peak point. It started interfering with my sleep. The startling, 3:00 A.M. wake-ups began, eventually followed by the telltale dry heaving. It was becoming an all-too-regular part of my daily life by this point.

It feels silly now to write about how much anxiety I had over planning my wedding. People do this all the time! I can't even tell you what it *was* that stressed me out so much. I don't think it was marrying Jeremy that was causing my anxiety, despite the eventual outcome of our marriage. I think that's just what anxiety is: unexplainable. It's not necessarily the cause that's the problem, it's the way your mind reacts to the things around you, even seemingly simple things that people do every day. It doesn't make sense; it's anxiety.

My wedding day was the kind dreams are made of: a sunset wedding on a cliff overlooking the Pacific Ocean. A small ceremony with only fifty of our closest family and friends. A reception at the Ritz-Carlton. A strapless Vera Wang gown. Really, everything was perfect . . . except for me.

A few weeks earlier, I had confessed to my doctor during a routine physical that I was having ever-growing anxiety about my impending nuptials. I still hadn't formally been diagnosed with Generalized Anxiety Disorder at this point, but the sleeplessness every night and dry heaving every morning was interfering with my daily life. I knew having wedding jitters was normal, but this felt like jitters magnified by a thousand. So my doctor prescribed Xanax to help me sleep leading up to the wedding with the advice, "Take half a Xanax thirty minutes before the ceremony." I had never taken any type of anti-anxiety medication before, but I felt desperate to get my nerves under control. I tested out the Xanax a couple of times in the weeks leading up to the wedding, to help me sleep and to make sure there were no side effects. I wasn't nervous to try this new medication, I was desperate to feel less out of control. The Xanax didn't stop the anxious thoughts from spinning inside my head, but I did notice some physical effects, like my shoulders relaxing. I never realized just how tensely (and high!) I held my shoulders until I finally relaxed them a little. While the Xanax wasn't a cure-all, it certainly did help.

So I took the Xanax to help me get through my wedding ceremony without passing out from my overwrought nerves. I tried to ignore the growing feeling of, "What is *wrong* with me that I can't get through my own wedding without medicating myself?" My stomach was churning with nausea, and I was so jittery, I wanted to crawl out of my own skin. What if I tripped walking down the aisle? What if I messed up my vows? Did I look happy or emotional? Or was all of my panic written clearly all over my face? It's a great irony that I spent my entire childhood performing in front of millions of people, and now, during one of the most important, on-display moments of my personal life, I couldn't hold it together.

My wedding day was such a perfect representation of the yin and yang of my emotions. I felt overwhelmed with love. I looked around the room and felt more supported by the people in my life than ever. At the same time, I looked around and felt suffocated by the spotlight. The first dances made me self-conscious about all the eyes boring into the back of my perfect updo. I loved sharing these incredible milestone moments with the people I loved, but at the same time I really wished Jeremy and I were alone so that so many people weren't watching us. It was a very, very strange juxtaposition of emotions.

I think a lot of brides expect to remember their wedding day as nothing short of perfection from the minute they wake up in a sun-filled room to the second they fall asleep in their new husband's arms. Heck, I wish *I* could remember my wedding day like that. And most of my memories *do* center on those blissful moments. But I would be lying to myself if I said I didn't remember those anxiety-riddled moments from my big day, too.

We wrote our own vows, and I cried while reading mine. I remember thinking about how we didn't have a microphone, and I didn't know whether to project louder so our wedding guests could hear me (once a performer, always a performer!) or just chill out and say my vows. I hated that I was worrying about all of these minor details instead of just enjoying the amazing moments. Maybe we should have just eloped so I wouldn't have had all this dumb performance anxiety swirling in my head.

Our pastor, Don, gave a speech about "the loneliest number." The saying goes: "One is the loneliest number." But Don's argument was that *two* is actually the loneliest number. When you are stuck in a marriage where you aren't connecting with your spouse, two can become lonelier than one. That speech was well thought out and sage advice at the time. But it's eerie to think about now in the aftermath of my divorce. Don was right; two really *is* the loneliest number.

After the ceremony, Candace told me, "That was the most beautiful wedding I've ever seen." And it really was. This became a great lesson in my life about milestones and living with anxiety. Things can look beautiful from the outside—and they can even be and feel beautiful inside. But the anxiety will always be there, lurking. Like a third person in our marriage, it was always there.

When the last of the wedding cake had been eaten, I felt a mixture of sadness that it was over and relief that our reception, and the wedding as a whole, had ended. But I didn't relax. I was still wound so tight with paralyzing anxiety that we didn't consummate our marriage that night. I simply could not calm down, relax, and enjoy my new husband. It's my single biggest regret of my wedding.

I woke up the next morning, my first morning as a married woman, and just like every morning for the past three months, dry heaved into the toilet.

This was my future.

Spending our first married year as students at the University of York in England was wonderful—just the two of us exploring a new country. And one of the biggest surprises was when we found out I was pregnant with our first child at the end of our year in England.

The greatest joy of my life has been raising my children. Those years when they were learning to walk and talk and explore their world, and I was home with them to soak up every sweet moment, are some of the happiest memories of my life.

Having my first baby rocked my world, in both a wonderful and challenging way. My firstborn, Tate, came out of the womb screaming. I felt similar: I was scared, too! All of the emotions of new motherhood were overwhelming: the excitement, the fear, the breathtaking love. I felt all of it.

Tate was so dang cute. He had a full head of hair with natural highlights that we joked looked like Ryan Seacrest's. He was colicky and cried a lot and did not like to sleep, so my new-mom euphoria was quickly replaced by anxiety. Breastfeeding was difficult. I was constantly worried—not knowing if he was hungry or if I was doing something wrong. In the hospital, I received multiple visits from multiple La Leche League consultants and multiple nurses who helped show me the proper way to breastfeed. Basically, my boobs were manhandled by almost everyone except the gift shop staff. I wasn't sleeping much, and my hormones were out of whack. At home, I felt like I was always "on," like I couldn't relax or let down my guard for even a second in case something bad happened to the baby.

Jeremy was a great new dad; he didn't seem plagued by worries, like I was. He became a master swaddler and could get Tate to sleep by rocking him on his side and shushing in his ear. Eventually, the three of us grew into our new roles as mom, dad, and not-always-crying son, and we got into a routine that was somewhat predictable.

But if I thought one child was challenging—ha! The transition from one kid to two when I had my daughter, Felicity, proved to be the greatest juggling act I'd ever faced. Where I had once felt relatively in control of my life, I now quickly realized I had exactly *zero* control. Over anything.

One afternoon when Tate was four and Felicity was one, I decided to tackle the small task of taking both kids to Target. They were acting unusually cranky and overtired, and I didn't really want to go, but I had a couple of returns to make. Plus, I had a raging sinus headache and we were out of Motrin. So off we went.

We escaped the war zone often referred to as a parking lot and reached our safe refuge inside the store. Of course, the first thing the children did was demand to ride in one of those obnoxiously large carts. You know, the ones with the ride-on attachment where they can sit? Seriously, this thing is like the RV of shopping carts. It has a turning radius of about two blocks. And I don't care who you are or how freakin' strong you are—NO ONE can push this cart with any smidgen of grace or without pulling a muscle. In fact, if you walk through a market and hear random deep, guttural grunting, I'll bet twenty bucks it's a mother struggling with one of these RV carts.

I tried to negotiate with the children: "Kids, we only have one thing we need to get. We don't NEED a cart." The children were having none of this and threatened to stage a sit-in protest right there in the Target entryway if they didn't get their RV cart. I waved my white flag and gave in, furthering my theory that four-year-olds could easily run the United Nations with their master negotiating skills.

We were inside Target for no more than sixty seconds—just enough time to reach the very back of the store—when Tate decided he wanted nothing to do with the RV cart. He stood, turned around, and attempted to swing from the bar (all while I was pushing it, mind you).

"I DON'T WANT TO SIT IN THE CART!" he yelled.

Okay, fine. Of course, now this meant Felicity didn't want to sit in the cart, either, because she just wanted to copy Tate. Now I was juggling two unruly children *and* an unruly RV cart.

Since we didn't even have anything in the cart, I decided to abandon it right there in the Christmas tree section and instead focus my efforts on chasing Felicity, who insisted on touching each and every glass ball ornament. After a few moments of being distracted, I noticed out of the corner of my eye that Tate was now pushing the formerly abandoned RV cart through the highly breakable glass ornament aisle. Another shopper's cart in his way? No problem! He plowed right through it and pressed on with the RV cart. Kid couldn't even see where he is going, but that didn't seem to slow him down one bit.

I managed to somehow stop him before a major disaster occurred and decided it was time to get the heck out of there. I extracted both children from the Christmas section, despite their high-volume protests. We picked up some frozen waffles and toothpaste and went straight to the checkout line, where the children proceeded to tear bags of chips off the shelves.

We got through the rest of the checkout line relatively unscathed, and I was about to make a beeline toward the car when Tate decided he needed to go to the bathroom. *Sigh*. Seriously?

Now, anyone who's had experience with kids will know that you cannot get through a public restroom with two small children without picking up at least a dozen communicable diseases. It's more attractive than a toy store, all that porcelain and ceramic! They physically cannot stop themselves from touching everything. An added benefit is that the only stall that fit all three of us was the handicapped stall, which meant the toilet seat was higher than usual, which meant Tate (who insisted on standing to pee) could not properly position and aim, so he did the only logical thing and rested his . . . parts . . . oh, so comfortably on the rim of the public toilet seat.

Free hepatitis A with any $20 purchase—today only! I could not get out of there fast enough.

We finally got back to the car to head home. As I pulled up to our driveway, I realized I never did get that Motrin I needed.

Another fun hallmark of parenting is all of the gastrointesti-
nal troubles that come with little bellies. Like when your kids
get rotavirus for the first time. Let me preface this by saying:
Do not read this next part if you are eating lunch . . . or even
sucking on a breath mint. In fact, if you have even the slightest
stomach sensitivities, you'll want to put down this book now
and walk away slowly.

For those of you who have not yet had the distinct pleasure
of experiencing this, rotavirus is a wicked little bug that, by all
accounts, is akin to having your stomach held hostage and repeatedly tortured. Rotavirus is NOT some innocent little flu. *It.
Means. Business.* And it is characterized by its very distinctive
and foul-smelling diarrhea. (I warned you not to read this.)

Tate came down with it at age two, exactly two days after
we attended a birthday party where the birthday girl threw up
in the middle of her own celebration. That should have been
my first warning. Poor Tate caught the bug next, and he was
absolutely miserable but oh, so brave. In fact, I have never in
my life met anyone who is so relatively *calm* about vomiting.
He didn't cry or scream or tense up; he just sadly threw up all
over whatever was in front of him—usually me. (On the opposite end of the puking spectrum, I'm a total stress case about
vomiting, my anxiety-induced dry heaving notwithstanding.
Give me a headache, give me a sore throat, give me a sprained
ankle, *give me anything*, but do not give me the flu. I will completely panic at the mere thought of vomiting. My entire body
will be sore for days after the illness has passed, just because I
was so damn tense about retching. But enough about me.)

On day three of the rotavirus, we took Tate to urgent care on the advice of our pediatrician to check his hydration levels and see if he needed an IV. Fortunately, he was still hydrated enough (how, I don't know) and didn't require a hospital stay. But the doctor gave him a shot of Tigan, an anti-nausea medication, to help keep the fluids down, as well as a prescription for suppositories.

Upon leaving urgent care, I was stoked about the suppositories. (Good ol' motherhood, right? When do you ever see "stoked" and "suppositories" in the same sentence?) Not only was Tate going to get the medicine he needed to feel better, but it wasn't medicine we would have to wrestle down his throat, only to have it spat out or vomited all up again, which was likely to happen even on a non-flu day. So I was cautiously optimistic about this new game plan.

That is, until we got home and attempted to insert the suppository. Let me tell you, you have not truly experienced the joys of parenting until you have stuck your pinkie finger up your child's arse. An added bonus is when your child arches his back, screams, and contorts his sphincter so the suppository continuously shoots back out the exit. THAT, my friends, is the definition of Unconditional Love.

Is anyone still reading this?

Ten minutes after we succeeded on the suppository front came the Big One, the One to Be Feared By All: The Rota-Poop. Let me preface this by saying Tate had not pooped in three days, so when the eruption finally occurred, not only do I think it registered on the Richter scale, I actually believe that every bug and spider in the house faced its immediate demise. It did not help when I asked Jeremy (who was second-in-command at the diaper table) to *sift through* the diaper in an attempt to locate the suppository and judge whether or not we needed to administer another one. Jeremy actually (are you ready for this?) drooled on himself. Literally—saliva came involuntarily dribbling out of his mouth. He later said that the experience reminded him of the gas chamber in Marine Corps boot camp, where you lose control over your bodily functions in an unconscious attempt to get the poisonous fumes out of your system. Oh. My. Gawd.

No, seriously, is anyone still reading this?

After the meds finally kicked in, Tate (and Jeremy and I) slept for three days straight. Welcome to parenthood!

Man, it's bittersweet. Those days felt *so* hard, and yet they were such a simple time. Easier, too, when I compare it to parenting my currently moody teenager and budding tween.

Back when I had energy and fewer gray hairs, I used to write my kids letters on their birthdays. I was never a scrapbooker, or even a good baby book filler-outer. But I could always write my feelings for my kids well, and that sort of became the scrapbook of their childhood.

This is an excerpt from a letter I wrote on Felicity's third birthday:

April 10, 2010

It's hard to believe it was three years ago when our sweet baby girl came into our lives. Birthdays are always a little bittersweet for me, but this one seems to be particularly so. You know that Britney Spears song, the one that goes, "I'm not a girl . . . not yet a

*woman . . ."? That sort of in-between-ness is where I
think Felicity is at age three—caught in between her
babyhood and her big-girl-hood.*

*She has grown so much the last year, and she's so
dang smart, I'm floored by the things she says every
single day. But she is STILL hanging on to some of that
baby chub! It's not a lot—mostly her little buddha belly
and little chubsters in her thighs—but it's just enough to
remind me that it wasn't so long ago that she was a
baby. And each month, she thins out a little more. She's
lost so much of her chubby cheeks. And I will be so sad
the day the chub finally disappears.*

*If I had to pick one word to describe this child, it
would be delightful. She is such a happy, exuberant
child; she is truly enjoyable to be around. I mean, yes
she has her moments of defiance and moodiness. But
generally speaking, she takes such joy in life and
learning and experiencing even such simple, everyday
things. It's contagious to be around her!*

*She loves being outside and exploring nature. She
loves all types of animals—particularly farm animals—
but she'll take any animal that happens to be nearby.
She loves visiting every playground within a ten-mile
radius of our home. The first thing she does is make a
beeline for the swings.*

*She takes special delight when she zooms down the
slides and ends up with staticky "witchy hair!"*

*This year has been particularly special because of all
the one-on-one time she and I have been able to have*

while Tate is at school in the mornings. One of her favorite things is going out on a lunch date with Mama to our favorite sandwich shop, and it thrills me to no end to look over our meal at her and see her little face peeking up over the table.

In September, she'll start preschool. People have started to ask me, "Oh my gosh, what will you do with two kid-free mornings a week?" But if I'm being completely honest, I don't want her to start preschool. I'm not sure if it's because she is my last child or if it's because she is extra-clingy, shy, and nervous around new people. But I suspect I'm sad mostly because I just don't want to give up any of these one-on-one mornings with her. I LOVE them. And I love that she is still an age where she just wants to be with me. I am her best bud right now, and I know it won't be that way forever. So I just don't want to let go of our mornings together. Not yet.

She still carries around her "sherts" (two of my old T-shirts) wherever she goes. If I try to take them away (even just temporarily), she'll say, "But they are special to me." God forbid I try to wash them—those things smell like old dirt and sweat. She will collapse into a crying heap if I put them into the washing machine.

"But Mama, they won't smell like you!" Heart. Melting. Now.

"Okay honey, you can have your stinky sherts for one more night."

She loves her big brother more than anything—it

*doesn't matter how much he taunts her or ignores her—
her love for him is infinite.*

*When she is upset and crying, often the first thing she
will ask for is, "Tate! Tate! Make a funny face!" (Of
course, this is only during the times in which Tate is not
the instigator of said tears.) Most days she spends just
trying to keep up with her big brother.*

*She wants to do or try whatever he is doing, be it
soccer or racing or scootering—she wants to do it all,
even though she's not as fast as him and still needs a
little extra help from Mom and Dad.*

*Her vocabulary is incredible, and by that I mean she
never stops talking. Ever. There are times when I have to
say, "Felicity, please stop talking for just five minutes so
that I can hear myself think!"*

*She is still extremely shy around new people, and
when they ask her questions, she often replies by
grunting, squawking, or meowing like a kitty cat. "How
old are you?" someone will ask, and she'll reply by
grunting, "MEHHHH." We get stopped all the time
by strangers who comment how cute she is, or how
captivating she is, or how beautiful her hair is. I don't
mean to sound like I'm bragging or boasting by saying
that—I'm usually taken aback whenever it happens. I
mean, I know I think she's effortlessly beautiful and
charming, because she's my child! But to hear others say
so, too, is . . . well, it's wonderful and humbling and
bewildering all at the same time!*

She is my beautiful, sweet, intelligent baby (big) girl. I love her so much, it's hard to put into words. When she asks me to cuddle and snuggle with her at bedtime, and when she curls up into the crook of my arm, the love is almost intoxicating. Sometimes I wonder if maybe the oxytocin still hasn't worn off even three years later. But no, I think it's just HER. She is simply delightful.

Happy Birthday, my sweet girl. I love you.

And when Tate turned seven, this was the letter I wrote about him:

April 30, 2011

Today, Tate turned seven years old. I look at him and still remember that mad, screaming face the doctor held up for me to see the day he was born. He still has that dimple on his face, the one that shows up every time he flashes that famous Tate smile.

He is happy, smart, and inquisitive. He works hard and plays hard. He does very well in school, and he is always a favorite amongst his teachers. His favorite subjects are "math and recess." He loves playing soccer, I think because it is one sport where he can justify his need to move around constantly! He is very good at soccer. He is not a star player (and doesn't need to be), but he is a very steadfast, dependable player.

He still thinks eating is a chore that does nothing except take precious minutes away from his LEGO playtime. He will still only eat foods that are within the beige color spectrum. The psychology behind how he

thinks about food is truly fascinating. One time, he saw
Felicity eating raisins and then pointedly told her, "You
know that raisins are grapes that have died, right?" No
wonder he dislikes food! Everyone told me he would
outgrow his picky eating habits when he started
elementary school. I am still waiting for that day.

There is a new word I would use to describe Tate
this year: resilient. He has endured tough situations
at school that no kid should have to put up with.
Unfortunately, I think it's becoming all too commonplace
at schools these days, and he is not the only one.
But what is NOT common is his reaction. And his
determination and resilience. I have seen him cry, fall
down, and pick himself right back up to keep going.
Even in the most stressful of situations, he never gave
up. Never even considered it.

"Proud" does not even begin to scratch the surface of
how I feel about him.

Seven years ago today, he made me a mother. On that
day, I thought my heart realized its full capacity to love.
What Tate has taught me over the last seven years is that
the human heart has no capacity for love. It grows.
Every single year.

Happy Birthday, my sweet Tate. I love you.

Raising babies who become little kids who become tweens,
who then morph unrecognizably into teenagers—and surviv-
ing all of this!—is one of life's greatest challenges. It's also the
most wondrous thing I've ever experienced.

These days, my kids are completely and utterly 100 percent unimpressed with my celebrity status. In fact, they are often annoyed by their mom being famous. I wish they weren't, but the fact that they aren't swayed by it is very refreshing. They don't give two hoots that I'm on television—especially Tate. He is completely mortified by his mother's fame. His version of Hell is me getting recognized in a Starbucks by kids he goes to school with. And yes, that has happened more than once. We never went back to that Starbucks after school. I do wish there was a bit more of a balance with Tate. I get that teenagers think everything their parents do is totally stupid. But I wish Tate could recognize that I work hard, and that my job extends beyond the studio (in that I still deal with "celebrity" even when I "clock out" of work) . . . and that, oftentimes, I'm just as bothered by it as he is. But I can be bothered by it while also *appreciating* it for what it is: a sign of success. It's a love-hate relationship, just like with most things in life.

Maybe he'll understand when he's older. (Note: In the time that it took me to complete this manuscript, Tate has come around and now gets a kick out of having a famous mom, because it impresses his teammates on the high school basketball team. Teenagers!)

As for Felicity, she watched *Fuller House* like any other twelve-year-old kid. She didn't pump me for information about behind-the-scenes tidbits. She liked coming to the set simply because of craft service and because she enjoyed hanging out with Mom and the other kids her age. Rarely did she actually watch the performances.

On occasion, I got the sense that she was aware that her

friends were impressed with my celebrity. And only on very rare occasions was I aware that she had bragged. ("This jacket I'm wearing is from Candace.") But I put her in line real quick after those instances. *Real* quick.

One day after picking her up from school, I discovered that she had been ripping my signature out of her homework agenda (which I sign every night) and trading it with kids in the cafeteria for chicken nuggets. She may not be impressed that Mom is a celeb, but she sure knows how to work it to her advantage! In case you're wondering, the going rate for my autograph was three chicken nuggets.

For the most part, I think she just liked being liked and wanted to fit in, but she did get irritated when some of her teachers kept asking her questions about me. Sounds like a pretty average kid to me.

While I do love motherhood with all that I am, my kids frustrate me on a daily basis. Let me not sugarcoat this entire parenthood deal! But those rare times that I'm able to strip away the aggravation and think about my kids less as "these things I am legally responsible for that require an insane amount of work" and more as *people* I've known since they took their first breath . . . well, I'm simply in awe. My kids have taught me to find joy in the smallest everyday things, like taking care of bugs and singing at the top of your lungs in the car. Or how Yogurtland really can be the thing that turns your day around. Or the healing power of laughter or a very well-timed fart during bedtime stories.

It's funny how love for your child evolves. I mean, you always love your children with the wholeness of your heart and self. But the way in which the love evolves as time passes . . . that is a part of parenthood I didn't anticipate.

When they're born, you love them simply because they exist. Because they are here, and because they are a part of you, forever.

As they grow to become tiny little toddlers, you love the way they talk and learn the rules of language. You love the little pudge on their thighs, their Frankenstein walk, and the smell of their soft skin.

And then suddenly one day, without warning, you wake up and they're kids. Real, bona fide, BIG kids! And you wonder, "When the hell did this happen?" They have lost their pudge and their funny little lispy way of saying certain words. You no longer have such a strong desire to smell their skin because . . . well, that distinctive "boy" aroma is now present and accounted for.

But still you love them—in some ways even more so, because you see the kind of person they're becoming, and it makes you proud. You are amazed at the intelligent things they say, at their ability to feel and understand the world around them.

Author Anna Quindlen describes the progression of tears as a sign of a human's progress: "The tears of a baby are often a reflex, for a toddler almost always the fruit of frustration or fatigue. The tears of a child begin to be the tears of knowledge." And she is so right.

You hurt when they hurt. You hurt when you see them struggling. You hurt because you suddenly realize you can no longer fix everything with a simple kiss and a Band-Aid.

And it is that deep ache and boundless pride that makes you realize: It isn't just their cuteness or their existence that makes you love them—it's their *personhood*. It is because of the person they have become and are still in the process of becoming that your heart bursts at the seams and you think, "How did I get so lucky to be your mom?"

Maybe it's the overall sense of mild delirium from lack of sleep. Maybe it's those surprise hugs that seemingly come out of nowhere. Or, maybe, I am simply filled to the brim by motherhood.

CHAPTER SEVEN

The Anxiety Beast

HOURS BEFORE THE SUN RISES to meet the day, my brain awakens.

For a fleeting second before I'm fully conscious, everything is fine. And then I remember. It all comes rushing back in one crushing tidal wave of nausea and malaise.

I am anxious. I am depressed.

My eyes are still closed. I don't even fully remember yet all of the reasons why I'm anxious and depressed. That will come. Right now, I'm in that in-between state of feeling awful and not being awake enough to remember why.

I desperately want to go back to sleep. I try to will myself back to sleep, simply so I don't have to face the day and feel the pain. Sleep is the only release I get. And even then, my nights are plagued by my anxieties and doomsday feelings. My body hurts; I wonder if it's from being tense all night with nightmares.

My eyes are still closed, but my brain is already racing. I can't get it to stop. I start mentally cataloging all of the reasons why I'm depressed.

A fight with my boyfriend the night before.

The fights I have with my children every single day over the same damn things, the things that drain the life out of me.

The emotional eating I did the night before, trying to make myself feel better.

The chronic dissatisfaction with the way I look.

The clutter in my home, which mirrors the clutter in my brain.

The news I read last night about fourteen kids dying in a bus crash, exacerbating my feelings that this is a terrible world to live in and tragedy will be inevitable in my life. I'm simply waiting.

The fact that my ex-husband divorced me and moved on so quickly. The fact that I still feel the loss of my complete family. Yet another one of my failures.

The fact that I can't get past any of these things, even years later. And it feels like I never will.

All of these jumbled thoughts swirl in my brain into one giant tornado.

My body is so tired and sore. I mentally criticize myself for being so weak. There is no good reason for my body to hurt this much.

The depression spreads over my entire body like a virus. I'm so drained. Every inch of me is taxed. I feel as depleted as if I'd run a marathon.

I don't want to die, but I don't want to live with this anymore.

My eyes flick open. My day begins.

*   *   *

I've had nervous habits and an anxious personality since I was very young. When I was a teenager who threw up on the mornings of performances or big tests, I thought that was normal. When I bit off all my nails into my twenties, I thought being anxious all the time was just a personality trait. When I was a bride needing Xanax to get through my wedding ceremony, I thought my anxiety was situational. "This will pass," I thought. "I just have a lot of stressful things going on in my life right now."

I didn't know, at the time, that what I had was a mental illness.

I didn't know it was diagnosable. I didn't know it was a condition that could be treated (not cured, true, but managed by treatment). I didn't know that anxiety and depression are like cousins, that the two are often intertwined, and that having one (anxiety) often leads to the development of the other (depression). And I certainly didn't know that forty million American adults suffer from some type of anxiety. I didn't know there was a tribe out there who could relate.

The "stress" in my life continued—or rather, my inability to cope with normal challenges in life left me in a perpetual state of worry and mental paralysis. The anxiety felt completely disconnected from my life, and I couldn't wrap my brain around the idea of accepting it. Why would *I* have anxiety? I had a wonderful, supportive family. I got excellent grades in school. I achieved a lot of success as a child actor, which provided me with cushy savings to fall back on if I ever needed to. I wasn't neglected, abused, or damaged in any obvious way. So where was this anxiety coming from?

In my naivety, I assumed I wasn't a candidate for an anxiety disorder. I didn't realize that anxiety does not discriminate against privilege or class or race or gender or life circumstances. It is an equal-opportunity mental illness, for lack of a better phrase.

I stressed my way through a challenging master's program at the University of York in England. New country + new people + culture shock + difficult academic material = a recipe for not sleeping, nor much eating. As I was getting ready to submit the final copy of my master's dissertation, two things happened within twenty-four hours of each other: I applied for my dream job back in the States, and I found out I was pregnant. Whaaaaaaaat? This was a curveball. Now I was anxious, nervous, nauseated, and dizzy, and I couldn't tell which were anxiety symptoms and which were normal pregnancy symptoms.

Pregnancy really did a number on both my body and my psyche. I felt worried every waking second of the day. About my dissertation. About my prospective job. About my pregnancy. About my future. When my anxiety is at its worst, my world closes into a pinhole-sized view, and it's all I can think about. It's a very overwhelming and devastating feeling, and very different from what I'd always assumed anxiety was (butterflies in my stomach before a speech). Tasks that once seemed easy and fun suddenly feel insurmountable. I can feel my heart pounding in my chest. It's kind of like the sensation you get when you're at the very top of a roller coaster, white-knuckled hands gripping the bar in front of you, about to plummet downwards. That adrenaline and fear kick into overdrive . . . but in the case of anxiety, there would be no letup. I was constantly in that white-knuckled state, holding my breath, gripped by the fear of the unknown. When you feel like that even in the absence of actual, present danger, *that* is anxiety.

I flew to Philadelphia to interview for that dream job: a position with Arcadia University's College of Global Studies as their southwest regional program manager. Scoring this job would mean I could work from home in Southern California and travel to areas in the Southwest to visit universities and promote study abroad to students. It would also mean a lot of international travel, which I already knew I loved.

I imagine many of you may be asking, "You're a celebrity; why are you getting a 'normal' job?" Truth be told: I would have gotten a "normal" job even if I could have lived off residuals from *Full House*. (The truth is, I couldn't—residuals don't usually add up to enough money to pay the bills.) That's just the type of person I am. I worked as a tour guide in college during summers, even though I was living with my parents and didn't "need" the money. It was more about routine and finding purpose and passions in life.

For the Arcadia University position, I interviewed with John, the director of enrollment management, and told him straight up, "I'm pregnant." I know everyone says this is the *last* thing you should tell a potential employer, but I had to be honest, almost like a Pavlovian response to all the stress and anxiety I was feeling. I couldn't handle the pressure of keeping my pregnancy a secret. It was all I could think about. I couldn't even focus on the questions John was asking me. So I blurted out my confession. John responded with a genuine, "Congratulations! How wonderful!" and then, a few days after the interview, he offered me the job. I guess Arcadia takes that "you can't discriminate against pregnant women" law quite seriously!

So, OMG, yay! I had my dream job, and I would be traveling so much and talking to students and everything I loved and . . . OMG I'M PREGNANT AND GOING TO THROW UP!

I threw up every morning of my pregnancy. I know morning sickness is a normal part of the first trimester, but in the back of my mind I kept wondering how much of it was my normal anxious morning routine of throwing up, and how much was morning sickness. Where did the anxiety symptoms end and the pregnancy symptoms begin?

I think the answer is that the two exacerbated each other. The hormones, the changes in my body, the anxiety—it all somersaulted right together into one big ball of distress.

I both loved my new job and dreaded it. I knew deep down that traveling and mentoring students were passions of mine. I had the perfect career, but I couldn't stop my brain from getting triggered and spiraling into an abyss of chronic worry. Even though I didn't know at this point that I was suffering from anxiety in a clinical sense, I knew what types of situations pushed my frayed nerves into overdrive, and I usually coped by avoiding those situations completely. But with this new job, I could not avoid these triggers. I traveled to new colleges every day (trigger). I met with deans of various departments every week (trigger). I made small talk with strangers all the time (trigger). *Why is this so difficult for me?* I became angry with myself. I was so lucky to have this job, and these weren't difficult tasks. It wasn't rocket science! Why couldn't I get a grip? Why wasn't my brain cooperating?

Then my boss announced that I would be going on a ten-day trip to Ireland to tour Irish universities and meet their deans, sort of like a "field research" trip so I would be able to learn more about Irish culture and education, then return home and talk to American students about study abroad in Ireland. What an awesome opportunity, right? My anxiety disagreed. My brain immediately went into panic mode. How was I going to survive this trip? I threw up every day, and on bad days it could go on for hours. I couldn't stand for more than thirty minutes without feeling dizzy, like I was going to faint—a common side effect of pregnancy, my doctor told me.

My OB-GYN prescribed me Zofran, an anti-nausea medication, to help with the morning (sometimes all-day) sickness and told me to wear compression socks to help with the dizziness. I did all of these things and somehow survived the trip, despite vomiting every day. But when I got home, my brain resumed spinning, and I spent what felt like every waking minute trying to get it to stop.

I started sleeping in the bathroom because I was dry heaving all night. I canceled my attendance at a work conference because I couldn't face it, calling to tell my boss I was "sick"—which I was. But I didn't tell him (because I didn't realize) that my inability to pull myself off the bathroom floor was a mental illness that created physical illness as a side effect.

I sat down with Jeremy one night and said, "I can't do this anymore. I have to make it stop." The baby was due in three months, and if I felt this anxious and out of my mind *now*, how awful would it be when I became a new mother and had a newborn to take care of? The travel, the stress . . . I felt like I had no other choice. Jeremy said he would support whatever I decided. I think he was just as frustrated with my inability to handle this job as I was.

The next day, I wrote my boss my resignation letter. As always, he was just as supportive that day as he was the first, when I told him I was pregnant. Still, I felt like I had let everyone down. Myself most of all.

Quitting my job did provide some immediate relief. The triggers and stressors of the job were gone. I felt like I could breathe enough to get my brain to stop spinning, at least temporarily, and focus on getting ready for the new baby. But I was still wracked with guilt and self-blame. I felt inadequate for not being able to handle a job and a pregnancy. I felt like there was something wrong with me, that I had to drastically change my environment by quitting my job in order to function in the world like a "real" person. I hated this part of me, but I felt helpless to change it.

A couple of months later, my beautiful son, Tate, was born. It was equal parts exhilarating and terrifying. Having your first baby is challenging and full of new types of stress. I'm sure my foray into new parenthood wasn't particularly different from any other new-parent scenario. But it sure *felt* more challenging than what I expected. Tate cried for what felt like six weeks straight. It was a Herculean task to get this baby to sleep. We employed the five S's (swaddle, shush, suck, side position, swing), and Tate required *all five* at all times. I remember burning out our vacuum because the white noise from the machine was the only thing that put this kid to sleep. I existed in a constant state of exhaustion. I just remember being tired. Very, VERY tired. The sleep deprivation plus the non-stop crying frayed my nerves like a wick burned to its end. I could never relax, even when the baby was sleeping. I was always on edge, just waiting for the next crying spell.

My second pregnancy proved to be considerably more challenging than the first. Everything was twice as hard. I was dealing with fatigue and morning sickness while also chasing a toddler around all day. My morning sickness (which lasted every day of all nine months) was so severe, I was diagnosed with hyperemesis gravidarum, which is much more extreme than typical morning sickness and requires a lot of monitoring to make sure you don't get severely dehydrated. Again, I wondered in the back of my mind, "How much of this is morning sickness, and how much of it is exacerbated by my ever-growing anxiety?"

My kids were born three years apart, which I thought would make life easier—the firstborn would be old enough to help out with the baby. Plus, I'd already had almost three years of experience with motherhood. I had this down to a science, right? Ha! Life with two small children was a whole 'nother story. Their needs were completely opposite of each other: One needed multiple naps; the other needed constant movement. One needed lots of social interactions and a never-ending string of playdates; the other had a chronic runny nose or cough and had to stay sequestered. My life was a spinning hamster wheel of diaper changes, potty training, picky eaters, bedtime routines. After six months, I felt like I'd reached a point where I was handling all of this pretty well . . . until one day, my world started spinning and I couldn't make it stop.

I can't exactly pinpoint *one thing* that led to my ultimate breakdown. Rather, I believe it was a collection of stressors, one piled on top of another, that slowly eroded away my ability to cope. Tate, like most preschoolers, went through a period of one illness after another: fevers, double ear infections, respiratory problems, stomach pain that we feared was a ruptured appendix. Illness on top of illness led to a trip to the ER. And then an overnight stay at the children's hospital. A lot of sleepless nights. A *lot* of worry and unknowns.

My children eventually got healthy, and life returned to normal. But I did not. Once I was finally able to exhale, I began having what would become a long series of extreme panic attacks.

I would wake up around 3 A.M. every morning, completely paralyzed and drenched in sweat, unable to move until the urge to vomit overwhelmed me so much that I would run to the toilet and heave. My mind was blank; I wasn't thinking about any one problem in particular. I just couldn't unclench my fists, shoulders, jaw, or mind. I felt panicked. Over what? I didn't know. But it felt like my heart was racing from the second I woke up. Sometimes, it felt like maybe my constantly racing heart was the thing that woke me up. And this continued every night, until eventually I stopped sleeping and eating. I lost a dramatic amount of weight in two weeks, putting me at an alarmingly unhealthy 98 pounds. My ability to function completely ceased, and I was unable to take care of the kids—or even myself. My husband knew these things were happening to me, but he didn't know why it was happening or how to help. I can hardly blame him. I had no idea myself.

Looking back, I knew I had struggled with anxiety (without having a clinical diagnosis yet) for most of my life, but only on a couple of occasions did it interfere with my daily living, and I would always seem to get back on track within a few days or so. This time was different—it was more severe than ever before. And the worst part was that *it wasn't going away*. The panic attacks continued and got worse. I became very depressed. I lived every moment in fear of being alone or being alone with the kids—not because I was afraid of harming them or myself (and trust me, every health professional I talked to asked me that question!)—but because I was afraid of my own emotions. I was afraid of the overwhelming distress that would grab hold of my brain and not let go. I mean, isn't that the very essence of depression? The inability to escape yourself?

So while I didn't want to harm the children, I wanted desperately to escape them. I wanted to leave them with a competent adult and run away as fast as I could for an indefinite period of time. I wanted them to be cared for properly, and I felt I was no longer the right person for the job. I was unable to feed them. I no longer knew how to play with them or relate to them. I saw them merely as a source of stress and anxiety that I needed so desperately to escape.

I eventually met with several therapists over the course of a few months, and they all unequivocally agreed that I was suffering from not only anxiety, but postpartum depression as well. This struck me as odd. I had thought postpartum depression was something that only happened right after the baby was born, and Felicity was almost nine months old by this point (and Tate was four). Apparently, as I learned, postpartum depression can strike at any time within the first year after birth. If I had known this information before my big breakdown, I might have sought treatment sooner.

At first, I coped by relying on others since I felt like I couldn't handle the day-to-day myself. My parents would come over every day to help me with the kids. Jeremy took time off work to stay with me as well, but he had a new job at a big law firm, and I felt like I was a big burden to him. So it was really my mom and dad who shouldered the responsibility of getting me through this tough time. Jeremy didn't understand what I was experiencing. I didn't see it back then, but this was the first foreshadowing of trouble in my marriage, as my therapist would later suggest. Jeremy wasn't a horrible or uncaring partner through this ordeal. I think he just didn't understand the anxiety and felt unsure of what to do, and since my parents were there, they did a lot of the heavy lifting.

My condition wasn't improving, and one day I called my parents at 5 A.M. and asked them to come pick me up because everyone was asleep at my house. I didn't want to be any more of a bother to Jeremy than I already felt I was, and I couldn't be alone or drive myself. I was literally frozen on my couch. My heart was racing. I was breathing so hard I was dizzy. I was dry heaving. I didn't know how I was going to survive the next five minutes of this, much less an entire day. The anxiety was suffocating me.

My dad picked me up and drove me to my parents' house.

Jeremy stayed home with the kids. And later that day, my parents packed up our belongings and moved all four of us into their house for what was the beginning of several weeks of nursing me back to health. Jeremy was fine with this arrangement. He had enough stress on his plate with his new job, so he was willing to do anything to get me healthy.

It was like being a child again. I couldn't take care of myself, and I needed my mom and dad. I didn't want to eat. They had to feed me. They would literally put toast or a bland turkey sandwich in front of me and demand, "Eat this." I would eat one or two bites, and eventually I had enough of an appetite to eat the entire sandwich. Baby steps.

My parents also forced me to go for a walk at a local park every day. I didn't want to leave my bed, and besides, *What good will walking do?* I thought angrily. But walking was one of the two requirements—along with eating— my parents insisted upon every day. So we would strap my daughter into her stroller, and my mom, dad, Tate, and I would walk for an hour. The combination of fresh air and endorphins was so therapeutic. (Another moment of foreshadowing: Four years later, I would discover that running can be my most effective therapy.) I didn't realize it while walking the neighborhood with my family, sometimes crying, sometimes in a daze, but I was slowly healing.

My mom and dad never once lost patience with me, even as I was spiraling. They never once doubted that I would get better. They told me they would help me through this, no matter how long it took. It's really quite incredible to think about what they did for me. Having a solid, reliable support system is what helped me crawl out of my dark hole and seek treatment. I needed someone to force me to eat, to take walks, even to shower, because I didn't have the energy or desire to do it myself.

It was right around this point that we all realized this problem was bigger than me, it wasn't going away, and I needed professional help. I didn't even know where to start seeking help; it all felt so overwhelming and foreign. Since I didn't know what professional to reach out to and I was paralyzed with indecision, my parents called my OB-GYN (also a family friend) at home. Years ago, he had given me his home phone number and told me to call him if I ever needed to. My parents dialed the phone for me and explained to my doctor briefly what was going on, then handed the phone to me. I didn't even know what to say, but my doctor was extremely supportive, extremely sympathetic, and asked me a series of questions. And then he prescribed me an antidepressant and an anti-anxiety medication.

I was initially resistant to the idea of medication; in fact, I agonized over it. I say "agonized" because there was (and still is, although to a much lesser extent) such a stigma surrounding mental illness and medication. Of course, this is ridiculous— mental illness is no different than any other type of illness; there is nothing to be ashamed of. But at the time, I didn't know anyone who took antidepressants. I wasn't ready to go there (emotionally), but my body was shutting down due to the effects of my debilitating anxiety. My children were losing their mother. I owed it to them, if no one else, to do everything

I could to fight through the anxiety and depression. So I filled the prescription.

I didn't take the medication right away. I still worried about whether it was the right course to take. But having anxiety so debilitating that I couldn't get off the bathroom floor was a strong indication that I needed to do something. The antidepressant (Zoloft) was safe for breastfeeding mothers, but at the time, the anti-anxiety medicine (Xanax) in the dosage I was prescribed was not considered to be safe while nursing. This was another factor in my reluctance to take the pills. I tried everything I could to find a way to keep breastfeeding, including talking to the pharmacist, calling a lactation consultant, and meeting with Felicity's pediatrician. And even the pediatrician, who is a huge breastfeeding advocate and a member of La Leche League, told me, "As much as I advocate breastfeeding, Andrea, in this case, your health is more important than breastfeeding." So I compromised. I pumped and dumped every day until the Xanax wore off. But that meant we quickly used up the frozen milk I'd saved in the freezer, and eventually we had to supplement with formula.

I don't think many people understand why this was so heartbreaking for me. Everyone said, "Andrea, give yourself a break and stop nursing." But stopping nursing was anything but a "break." Sure, I would have to start making bottles and cleaning bottles and trying to get a baby who'd never had formula to suddenly start taking this foreign substance, which was a lot more work than breastfeeding, but this wasn't even my main concern. More importantly—and this is the part that I think a lot of people don't really get—the issue was the loss of the only real connection I felt I had left with my baby. I could not relate to this child at all. I wanted to escape her. Nursing was the one way I could still connect with her, and in a way that only I could do. I was devastated at the thought of losing that connection with her.

It was all kind of a moot point anyway. I was so malnourished by then, my body was producing very little milk. I remember three very long nights of the baby waking up hungry and crying every hour, and my body being unable to produce what she needed. My body and my mind felt broken. It was an agonizing decision in the moment to give up breastfeeding, but I realize now that it was my first step toward becoming the healthy, present mother that I wanted to be.

The Xanax helped, at least in the short term. It would help me become unparalyzed and enable me to get out of bed and start moving. But it would wear off after about four hours, so I would have to take another dose or only have a short window of time in which I could function. It wasn't a long-term solution. The antidepressant Zoloft, I learned, would take at least three or four weeks before it would get into my system and start working. So although the edge was taken off, I still wasn't functioning at 100 percent. I still didn't recognize myself.

At this time, I was also searching for a therapist to help me work through all that was happening. I met with a total of three before I found one with whom I clicked. The first one was nice, but she was very quiet and didn't really give me much feedback. I don't know if this was deliberate on her part to make me uncomfortable and see how my anxiety works, or if she just was at a loss for words. But I needed that two-way conversation with someone who could tell me what the hell was wrong with me.

She did, however, provide one useful piece of information. She kept asking me to describe all of Tate's illnesses and she kept repeating, "Wow, that sounds really scary. That must've been scary for you." I wanted to shake her and say, "Yes, the illnesses were scary. But that was NOTHING compared to the emotional warfare that is taking place in my brain. Why don't you get that?" The illnesses I had handled fine. So why was I falling apart now—even though everyone was healthy? She said it is very common for anxiety and depression to occur *after* the traumatic event. In the moment, you hold it all together just to get through. And it's not until afterwards that you finally allow yourself to process and then fall apart. Okay . . . so that made sense. Now I knew what could have triggered my anxiety and that what I was experiencing was not unusual.

The second therapist I saw was a psychiatrist, and she was awful. Seriously awful. She would not look me in the eye; she was completely devoid of any sort of emotion or sympathy. All she did was ask me questions and write on her stupid pad. I wanted to crawl out of my skin. I almost left in the middle of the session. I think she actually made my anxiety worse. I knew she wasn't the right fit when she asked me these two questions: "Can't you just get some help with the kids?" And, "What are your kids doing that stress you out so much?" Um, yes, I *can* get help with the kids, that's not the point. And it's not anything the kids are doing. They're great kids. It's *me* that's the problem. *My* inability to cope with normal events. If she didn't get that, she obviously didn't get me or my problem. I couldn't get out of there fast enough.

This led me to meet with a third therapist—a recommendation from my OB-GYN—and at last I found someone who felt perfect for me. She is incredible, kind, and compassionate, truly a wonderful person and professional. She is someone I could see myself being friends with if it weren't for that patient-professional barrier. I feel that comfortable with her. And she is a mother of two herself, so that helps. She taught me about anxiety in the clinical sense—how my anxiety presents itself, and what is happening inside my brain and body. Simply learning about the illness helped me understand and start to accept it much more. She also taught me coping strategies, like breathing and visualization. She encouraged me to be active every day, like the walking I started with my parents. She illustrated how vital it was to get proper sleep and nutrition not only for the health of my body, but for my brain.

My story proves that finding a therapist is not always a smooth process. People don't realize that, in strange way, it's sort of like dating. You have to shop around a little to discover what you need and don't need in a therapist. You may have to meet with several before finding someone you click with and trust. It takes time, but eventually, you will find the right one. And then you will live happily ever . . . or, well, you will begin to *heal*. And that is the most important, and biggest, first step.

The ironic thing is I was so fortunate to be surrounded by this incredible support system—my husband, my parents, my OB-GYN, and my therapist—yet I'd never felt so alone in my life. This is not to discount all the support everyone was giving me, but I felt that no one could possibly understand what I was going through, nor could anyone grasp the intensity of the hopeless thoughts churning through my head. Nobody had ever felt this way before, right? I just didn't see how it was possible. That's how intense my anxiety and depression was.

I was also convinced, *utterly* convinced, that it was never going to end, that I would never get better. My parents and therapist told me, "You *will* get better, you just have to have patience." But I didn't believe them. It had been months with no improvement. Having "patience" was a joke; I was living my life minute by minute, counting down the seconds until I could (hopefully) pass out from exhaustion. Sleep (when I could manage to get any) was the only respite from my unrelenting anxiety.

Part of the work I did with my therapist, in addition to rethinking food and exercise, was relearning how to relate to my children, weird as that may sound. I spent time with one child at a time, playing with them, hugging them, telling them I loved them. Slowly, as I began to find my footing again, I started to laugh and enjoy being their mom again. I felt a strange combination of guilt (that I had dropped so far off the radar as a mother) and relief (that I was healing and finding myself again).

And slowly, I did start to feel better. I'm not quite sure when it happened, but I think it was during one of our daily walks through the park. The day suddenly didn't feel so long, overwhelming, or dreadful. I heard birds chirping in the park for the first time and thought, *Wow, that sounds beautiful.* The sun actually felt good on my face; in fact, I was noticing the sun for the first time after months of what felt like overcast days. For the first time in months, I had the desire to eat and go for a walk instead of being forced to do these things. My spirits were slowly lifting.

The anxiety attacks continued, but they were getting less intense and were primarily limited to the mornings instead of all day. It took about three months before I was able to get up in the morning without heaving into the toilet, but for the time being, it was a wonderful feeling to wake up and not dread the day.

I reached a place where I really and truly loved being a mom to my kids again. I felt capable again. When I would have previously dreaded being alone with my children, I now relished it. We started visiting aquariums and the library again; we spent a lot of time outside walking in parks and feeding ducks and exploring new playgrounds and enjoying the sun on our faces. Seriously, does it get better than that?

It still felt weird taking medication to manage my brain even though it was helping me so much, which just goes to show how powerful and dumb the stigma can be. I remember a time during this period that I went to the doctor with a cold and congestion, and the nurse asked me to list any medications I was currently taking. Suddenly, I felt very self-conscious. That was the first time I had to publicly admit that I was taking an antidepressant and an anti-anxiety medication. Would the nurse judge me? I felt like I needed to qualify it, like saying, "I'm okay, really. I just need a little . . . help." I doubt the nurse even batted an eye. But it felt weird to admit that I needed help, like I was admitting that I was weak. I knew in my head that I wasn't weak, nor would I *ever* think that about someone else, but that's how it felt at the time, being a newbie with a fresh diagnosis of Generalized Anxiety Disorder and Depression.

After the diagnosis, I spent a long time avoiding friends and sitting with this huge secret hanging over my head: I HAVE ANXIETY. I felt ashamed. My friends started to ask why I was so quiet. They would ask about my day or life. I would have no response to even a simple, "How are you?" "Fine," was about as much as I could muster. The anxiety was all I could think about for a really long time. The stress of keeping my secret was becoming too heavy to bear. It felt like a shameful, dirty little secret that I was hiding.

I wrote my story and posted it on Facebook for my friends and family to read, so they would know that I had gone through this huge, seemingly bigger-than-life thing, and that it was a part of me. The response I received? Overwhelming. I received love. I received acceptance. I received so many messages of, "Me too." All of the things I feared—ridicule, criticism—never materialized.

For the first time in a very long time, I felt whole.

CHAPTER EIGHT

The Diagnosis
...Now What?

I SPENT SO MANY YEARS WISHING I didn't have this illness. I spent so many years just wishing I could *will* the anxiety away. But I couldn't. I couldn't make it go away. And I hated that about myself. The anxiety was such a large part of me, which means I hated a lot of *me*. I hated that I felt powerless against it for years.

It took a lot of therapy to simply understand this mental illness enough to know what was happening to me, why I felt the way I did, and why my body and mind reacted the way they did. And it took me even longer to acknowledge it, accept it as a part of me, and let go of the hatred.

It was that acceptance that led to the beginning of recovery and healing and the path to a happier life.

I have been with my therapist for over ten years now. We don't have a schedule of when we meet; it all depends on the season of my struggles. When I'm in a period of high struggle—depression, not sleeping, dry heaving—we meet every week. When I'm in a period of lower struggle, we meet twice a month. When I'm not struggling with anything in particular, we meet once every few months, sort of like doing routine maintenance on a car. Ya gotta stay tuned up in order to function in the long term!

I have benefited so much from therapy that I sing its praises all the time. I feel so strongly about its merits that I recommend it to everyone. And I mean *everyone.* My belief is that there is not a single person on this earth who wouldn't benefit from therapy, mental illness or not. We all need to prioritize our health, both physical and mental, and we could all use tools for self-examination and self-improvement. When we feel right with ourselves, we create a better environment for everyone around us. I wish I lived in a country that prioritized mental health more so that therapy would be accessible to its citizens on a regular basis, like physical health checkups. I wish mental health care was affordable, accessible, and encouraged for everyone. It is *that important.* What good is a healthy body if our brains are not just as healthy?

My therapist taught me a lot about anxiety and why my body and brain react the way they do to stress. One of the first topics we tackled was my dry heaving. It is the most telling sign that I am slipping and the anxiety is getting the better of me. *Why does this happen? What a bizarre symptom,* I thought.

It turns out that chronic dry heaving, gagging, vomiting, or nausea are common symptoms of anxiety. Have you ever gotten butterflies in your stomach before a big test or speech? That is a signal that your body is gearing up for a fight-or-flight situation, and it starts producing more adrenaline than usual. Often-times, this can be a good, even healthy, response because it keeps you on your toes and gives you the boost of energy you need to perform that test or speech well. But when it becomes chronic, or interferes with your daily functioning, it's a prob-lem.

My therapist explained that I carry most of my stress and anxiety in my stomach (other people may carry it elsewhere). My adrenal glands start to pump an excessive amount of adrena-line into my body. My constant anxiety is misinterpreted by my brain as danger. Even if there is no danger present, it doesn't matter; my fight-or-flight response is triggered. The tension and stress disrupt the stomach's normal function, which in turn causes nausea. My body is in constant fight-or-flight mode when I'm in a period of high anxiety, and then, over time, I can't shut it off. It's the reason why I would wake up early in the morning—my brain could not relax—and why I would spend the first hour of each day dry heaving into the toilet. It became a vicious cycle: The anxiety would cause the dry heav-ing, and the dry heaving would cause more anxiety.

The key was finding a way to break the cycle by managing the anxiety, but learning how to manage the anxiety was the hard part. I found a variety of methods that helped me. Be-cause my anxiety is so rooted in my gut, I need to make sure I eat several small meals a day so my stomach is never empty. (An empty stomach causes stomach acids to build, which causes more nausea, which is the *last* thing I need.) A protein-filled snack every night before bed, maybe cheese or nuts, keeps my stomach full as long as possible, which helps me stay asleep and curbs those early-morning bouts of nausea that make me rush to the bathroom.

Getting enough sleep needs to be a priority. This is hard when you have young children, but chronic lack of sleep raises the stress hormone cortisol, and I was desperately trying to *lower* my stress levels. So, back then, that often meant I would go to bed when the kids went to bed—early! It meant I couldn't stay up late to get stuff done around the house or watch my favorite TV shows, but I gladly accepted those consequences if it meant I was going to feel better all day. It's amazing how much getting good, regular sleep affects your mood. I know that seems like a no-brainer, but after sacrificing sleep for so long in order to fit more into the day, living on less sleep quickly becomes the norm (and consequently, so does moodiness and exhaustion). Going to bed early is now one of my favorite things in life.

I also learned that alcohol is a depressant, so I tend to avoid it. Actually, wait—that's not entirely true. I'm not proud to admit that I've used alcohol as a crutch to help me stumble through my anxiety, but I promised you transparency, so here it is. Small talk still renders me panic-stricken. If we're chatting and I suddenly excuse myself for no apparent reason, there's a 100 percent chance that I need to escape because the stress of just chatting is too difficult for me to bear for any lengthy stretch. I actively avoid situations where small talk is likely to occur. Grocery store checkout lines? I'm now the world's biggest champion of grocery home delivery. Haircuts? I put them off as long as possible. Social gatherings with people I don't really know? I head straight to the bar.

Alcohol dulled the edge of my anxiety. Alcohol suddenly made me confident and witty and loquacious. Alcohol made me less aware of the insecurities my brain wrapped around so tightly. You know what else I've learned? That alcohol undoubtedly increases my anxiety and depression the morning after. Those hangovers after a fun night out aren't just about dehydration and needing more water. The alcohol actually disrupts the balance of chemicals in your brain, which affects your thoughts, feelings, and moods. I was never an alcoholic or even a binge drinker; I just learned that alcohol and anxiety are not a good combination for me. A glass or two of wine now and then can be a treat, but like everything in life, it needs to be about moderation.

It also took me a long time to realize that all of those qualities that I longed for—to be confident and witty and charming— already exist inside of me. The anxiety clouds those qualities, yes . . . but they are there. I just need to be willing to tolerate the uncomfortable feelings of anxiety and reach past them to locate those positive qualities. But I know now that they are inside there, somewhere!

Running also became central to my recovery. Much of that was simply because of the physical benefits of endorphins. I was never a runner before, but a bunch of friends were signing up for a half marathon in Disneyland, and sometimes peer pressure gets the best of me. I never expected to love running the way I do, but it came at a time in my life when I desperately needed it. I've devoted an entire chapter to running, one of the loves of my life, but I want to address it here as well, specifically in terms of how it helps me cope with mental illness. It has been a total game changer.

Running creates endorphins, which in turn boost higher levels of serotonin. Serotonin is an important chemical inside your brain that regulates your mood, appetite, sleep, etc. If you have low levels of serotonin, you are more likely to become anxious or depressed. Running (or any heart rate–boosting exercise) is a natural serotonin booster.

But in addition to the physical and mental benefits of running, I was also experiencing emotional benefits. I was strengthening my body and my mind. I was conditioning myself to think, "If I can survive an eighteen-mile training run, I can survive a lot of hard things in life." I began to look forward to that "mood boost" each day when I ran. Even if I was in the throes of a particularly awful day, I knew I would feel better if I ran. So I did.

The spinning that ordinarily filled my head started to quiet. I felt invigorated and filled with a sense of hope—the very opposite of depression. Everything felt lighter.

I was also starting to feel a sense of peace that I hadn't felt in a very long time. I think yogis call this "flow"—the sensation that feels as if you're exactly where you're supposed to be, doing exactly what you're supposed to be doing, at exactly the right time. I think it's this magical combination of "flow" and endorphins and confidence that creates the famous "runner's high."

The running became a form of moving meditation for me. My therapist had told me about the benefits of meditation, the act of quieting the noise in my head, finding mental clarity, and achieving emotional calm. The running had such a rhythmic stability to it: the sound of my feet hitting the pavement, over and over again. The sound of my breathing, the air going in through my nose and out through my mouth. In and out, in and out. The rhythm of running allowed my mind to quiet, to contemplate my place in life. Oftentimes, I would reach a state in which I was completely unaware that I was running, lost in a daydream-like state. Then, when my run was over, I felt a profound sense of calm and mental clarity. Problems that seemed enormous prior to my run suddenly seemed manageable. As a contributing editor for *Runner's World* magazine, Kristin Armstrong, said in an interview, "There is something magical about running; after a certain distance, it transcends the body. Then a bit further, it transcends the mind. A bit further yet, and what you have before you, laid bare, is the soul."

The concept of meditation, or mindfulness, is to focus on the immediate present rather than the past or future. This skill can be extremely useful for an anxious person, especially one who constantly worries about the future or ruminates about mistakes made in the past. In this sense, running is a lot like meditation; you need to stay present in the moment, at whichever mile you're at. This is common advice for running a race: "Run the mile you're in." What this means is that you can't be fretting about mile twenty of a marathon if you're only on mile two. Run the mile you're in: If you're on mile one, keep your brain focused on mile one and warming up your legs. If you're on mile twenty-two, focus on conserving enough energy to finish the race strong. The same advice goes for life: Try to stay present in the *now* so you won't get so worked up about the future.

Meditation also teaches us that thoughts are just that: *thoughts*. They are not "you." So when I'm having anxious thoughts, it's helpful to recognize them as thoughts and emotions that are separate from my identity. It's being *aware* of these anxious thoughts, but not judging them as pleasant or unpleasant. They're just thoughts—they come and go and change throughout the day. The more I practice this, the better I'm able to let these uncomfortable thoughts exist and pass without spiraling out of control in my head. I'm able to make peace with my thoughts. (I highly recommend an app called Headspace for learning how to accept the ebb and flow of thoughts.)

After ten years of therapy and self-help, I no longer dry heave when I'm having an anxiety attack. My anxiety still manifests in other ways (like biting my nails—people give me such a hard time about it. I wish they knew that it's not something I *want* to do; it's just a symptom of my illness). But over time, I've learned coping strategies to live with my anxiety. I run. I meditate. I prioritize sleep. I know and can anticipate my triggers. I know I need time alone more often than other people in order to reset, so I turn down a lot of social invitations. Some days, my anxiety is so high that I can't leave the house, so I end up skipping birthday parties or friends' special events. I have a lot of guilt over that and sometimes feel like I'm a bad friend. But I try to give myself grace during those moments and know that my anxiety won't be that bad forever; it's just a dip. I know I will never be able to get rid of my anxiety completely. Unfortunately, it just doesn't work that way, and it will be with me for life. But I can live alongside it and not let it run my life.

As I've mentioned, one of the hardest things for me as a card-carrying member of the "Anxiety and Depression Club" is the question of whether or not to medicate.

That first time I took medication, I was in the very deep throes of postpartum depression and having trouble with basic functioning, like eating and getting out of bed. So there was no question at that time: I was in a hole and needed medication to help me climb out.

Since then, my relationship with medication for anxiety and depression has been on-again, off-again. There have been times when it's clear that I need it to function in a healthy way, so I'll stay on it for twelve months and then go off it. Other times, I'll go years without taking any anxiety or depression medication, and I'll feel just fine.

Like many things in life, these periods of anxiety and depression are seasons that come and go. And I try to take my life one season at a time, adjusting according to my needs.

I should add that *every* time I make a change to my medication—starting, stopping, changing dosage—I am always communicating with both my therapist and my psychiatrist (who prescribes my medication when I need it). I *never* make a change in my mental health habits without telling someone first. That way, if I ever end up on the bathroom floor again, sobbing and dry heaving for hours, my loved ones will know why.

There are many people for whom taking medication is not a question. They need to do so every day, period. And regardless of who you are and whether you need to take a pill every day, or just sometimes on an as-needed basis—I stand up and applaud *all* of us for being proactive about our mental health.

My relationship with these drugs has been complicated during the past few years. It hasn't always been quite so clear whether or not I should be taking them. There are a lot of questions and doubts that linger in my mind. The unfortunate reality is that most depression and anxiety medications have unwanted side effects. Some make you feel numb; not profoundly happy or sad any longer—you just don't feel much at all. Some make you gain weight. Some kill your libido. And some come with all of the above.

For me, these side effects created a love-hate relationship with the pills. I was grateful that the pills kept me out of that hole. But I *hated* the side effects. I hated feeling dependent on taking pills to feel "normal." I hated gaining twenty-plus pounds every time I had been on the drugs for several months. I hated feeling like I wasn't in control of my own body. I hated feeling like I only had two choices:

1. Live with very unwanted side effects.
2. Risk falling back into the hole.

I often seem to reach a point where my resentment of the side effects becomes greater than the benefits of the drug. I feel capable, but not necessarily happy. I feel fat. I feel at a loss. Most of all, I feel like I want to take back control of my body. But I'm still left with that lingering, perpetual question mark. Can I manage it on my own? *Should* I manage it on my own? Can I be happy without the assistance of a pill?

I ask myself these questions more often than I care to admit.

My knowledge and feelings about anxiety, medication, and coping strategies are always evolving, as I'm always learning new things. But I think, after more than a decade of actively managing my anxiety and depression, this is my personal conclusion: Medication can and will save your life. But medication by itself is not a quick cure-all. I cannot rely *solely* on medication to manage a mental illness.

Antidepressants and anti-anxiety medication are wonderful things. They can get you out of deep, dark ruts, and they can save your life. I am grateful for these medications that pulled me out of a slump that I couldn't get out of myself. For me personally, it was the *combination* of medicine and those lifestyle changes that turned my life around. Educating myself about anxiety and depression was the first step. Changing my diet and sleep patterns was the next. And incorporating running into my everyday life became the clincher. The running has become my most powerful antidote to anxiety. The medications made me feel *less*—less sad, less depressed. But the running made me feel *more*—more resilient, stronger, happier.

My therapist used the analogy of a diabetic: A diabetic must take insulin every day in order to stay healthy. They don't just take insulin when they remember or when they're having a bad day. Diabetes, and the management of it, is a lifestyle. So are anxiety and depression. If I want to fight it and remain healthy, I have to incorporate *all* of my strategies—medication, running, proper nutrition, meditation—into my everyday life. Even when I'm too busy or don't want to. It's not optional, it's a lifestyle.

It's actually very empowering to think about: *I* have the power to change my life. The medication can and did help. But *I'm* the one who sat in the driver's seat and took control of my life, one (literal) step at a time.

One of my favorite running shirts (created by my friend and fellow runner, Dorothy Beal) displays the motto: I RUN THIS BODY. At first glance, it might appear rather vain and braggy. But the double meaning is what makes me love this shirt. It's about taking control. *I* run this body. Not a diagnosis. Not a pill. Not shame. *Me.*

There is no antibiotic for anxiety; it is a mental illness. It will always be a part of me, but it will not always *rule* me. I've taken the power back.

I'll always have bad days and slumps and periods of struggle. But I feel that I'm equipped with the tools and the knowledge to fight it. To fight for getting *me* back.

I can feel now when I'm slipping into a bad place. I know when I need to force myself to take a step back and analyze: *What's going on here? What's triggering me into this episode? Is it something fairly easy to fix, like lack of sleep or self-care? Is it seasonal? Is it something in my personal life that I'm not coping with well?*

I don't have all the answers. But I have awareness now. I'm not going into this battle unarmed ever again. I have my arsenal of equipment to help battle the anxiety so it doesn't get the best of me. So the best of me *stays* with me.

I spent so long suffering in silence out of fear of appearing weak. When you're in the throes of anxiety and depression, when you're stuck in that deep, dark, painful place, it feels like you have no options. It feels like you will be stuck there forever. It feels helpless. It's a shame that we don't discuss mental illness in this country the way we discuss, say, cancer. It's perfectly acceptable to share a physical illness with one's peers (or the world, for the famous among us), and in return, those suffering get love, support, and sympathy. This isn't always the case with mental illness, and I find myself over and over again asking why. I hope we will one day get to the point where someone's diagnosis of anxiety, depression, or any other mental illness is met with a similar response to those with a physical illness. Maybe then those who are suffering will feel less alone. Maybe then we can truly start to support those quietly battling a chemical imbalance in their brains—something that is not their fault any more than cancer or a chronic illness would be.

Here's what I want you to come away with, if nothing else from this book. Please remember this: *You don't have to suffer in silence.* You are not weak. Talk to someone. Share what you're feeling. It is not shameful; it is *human* to want to share how we feel.

People called me brave when I shared my essay on depression for *InStyle*. I appreciate the compliment, but it also makes me ache for others who want to open up and be honest about their mental health but don't feel "brave" enough. We shouldn't *have* to feel like we have to suit up and be "brave" in order to share our struggles. Mental health struggles are common and not talked about openly enough. They are part of the human experience. We have come a long way toward creating open discussions about mental health, but there is still a stigma that exists out there. I want to live in a world where we can feel free to talk about the unpleasant parts of our lives, the parts that don't make it into the social media highlight reels, and not feel judged or shameful or self-conscious. How freeing would that be? We don't have to be brave; we just have to be *honest*.

As I'm writing this, the world has just learned about the death by suicide of celebrity chef Anthony Bourdain, which comes only a few days after the news of the death by suicide of fashion designer Kate Spade. It has become almost a knee-jerk response to post the hotline number for suicide prevention, along with messages encouraging people to reach out. And these hotlines and messages are very important. But part of what depression does is paralyze your ability to reach out. Telling people to "reach out" or "get help" only goes so far. A depressed person isn't *afraid* to ask for help; they are unequivocally convinced that there is *no such thing* as "help." They don't believe in their ability to feel better. Period.

I can tell you that during my deepest, darkest moments, I would personally have never called a hotline number. Asking for help from a stranger was the last thing I wanted to do. I felt weak and ashamed about my condition. But I was fortunate that I had supportive people in my life who recognized my pain and identified my need for help. They noticed when something felt off about me and spoke up. Thank God they understood my paralysis, my need for someone I trusted to step in and help by making that first phone call *for* me. It made all the difference. But not everyone is so fortunate. Everyone experiences their depression differently, and I'm so grateful that a hotline is there for those who will use it. But there are others who won't have the capability or desire to reach out. So here is my plea: If you are NOT depressed and you see someone struggling, *you* reach out to *them*. Stop and take notice of the people you love. Look into their eyes; listen to their words. And don't be afraid to speak up. It is our duty as members of the human race living on this same planet together to help each other and break the isolation that is depression.

Dear Evan Hansen (along with *TIME* magazine and Philosophy's Hope and Grace Initiative) created a campaign during May's Mental Health Awareness Month that challenged people to add one simple word to the question, "How are you?" That word was "really." It changes the sentence from merely a formality to a meaningful question that shows someone you care. "How are you, really?" Don't just tell me "fine," tell me what you're struggling with. Tell me something that made you feel good today. Tell me something that you have been afraid to say out loud.

I asked this question on my Twitter account, and the responses I received were overwhelming. I replied to every single one, not out of duty or obligation, but because hearing about so many others struggling helped me process my own struggles. I didn't have answers or solutions for anyone. I just wanted to tell people "I hear you. Your feelings are real." Sometimes you don't need an answer, you just need to feel *heard*. Sometimes you just need to know someone sees you. Sometimes you just need someone to acknowledge that your pain exists.

So many of us are struggling in isolation. Opening up an

honest dialogue about our mental health shows that we are not alone in this journey. We're all in it together.

Talk to someone. Anyone. If you aren't ready or able to see a therapist, talk to a close friend. Talk to *me*. I want to hear your story. I am not a mental health professional, and I don't have all the answers. I can't promise you that it will be easy. But I have compassion for others who struggle like I do, and I've learned that sharing your story is the first step toward releasing the power that the shame holds over you. Talking about it is the first step toward living a better life. For all those people who shared their own stories of struggle and survival with me, saying that my story made them feel a little less alone in this world: Please know that you have done that for me in return. Thank you.

There is an enormous tribe of us out there. And we are a tribe: We share a commonality. We don't look alike, we aren't related, we fall across all social and socioeconomic backgrounds. We are single, we are married, we are mothers, we are child-free, we are celebrities, we are everyday people, we are extroverted, we are silent, we are loud.

But we are ONE. Let's stand up for each other.

CHAPTER NINE

Surviving Divorce

OHHHHHH BOY. I HAVE BEEN AVOIDING writing this chapter for as long as I possibly could. Literally, this is the last thing I'm writing in the whole of my book. In fact, I considered simply titling this chapter "DIVORCE" and then leaving the rest of the pages blank. It's hard to revisit a time period I would rather forget.

My divorce was without a doubt the most painful thing I've ever gone through. It was so painful, I've never talked about it publicly. And I'm not going to "tell all" or sling mud or throw shade at Jeremy, because *what is the damn point of that?* It's not productive, nor is it graceful. But I did walk away from this complicated and arduous experience with some lessons and perspective that I believe are worth sharing.

The night of the dreaded Talk was the single worst night of my life. Even counting my anxiety-induced breakdown, it was the only time in my life that I remember feeling completely out of control of my every possible human emotion, expression, and response. And I mean, I *could not control* any of the tears, guttural cries, hyperventilating. I would liken it to a panic attack, but it was more than that. Worse than that. I was so scared, I couldn't even *breathe*. People describe having an out-of-body experience and simply watching themselves from above. And that's exactly what it was. It was like my brain shut down to protect itself, and I was merely watching all of this happen to me, unable to believe it was happening or control any of the horrible feelings or thoughts racing through my body.

I still have the couch that I sat on that night. Dammit. I loved that couch. And now I hate that couch. It's *such* a comfortable couch, I've never found another piece of furniture that compares. But it is also forever associated with the worst memory of my life. That damn couch.

The Talk was essentially the culmination of years of not prioritizing our relationship. Of letting kids and parenting dominate our home rather than protecting the rock that a marriage is supposed to be. I don't think my marriage ended due to one particular thing, but an awful, perfect storm of factors that slowly, methodically broke us down. I knew the Talk was coming, yet I didn't want to have it.

The day before was Mother's Day. We went for a family hike, and the tension in the air was suffocating. Jeremy was so cold toward me and refused to take my hand when I tried to hold his. Fear started to settle inside my chest. I guess I was in denial that things had gotten so bad, and I was hoping, denial turned on high, that the Talk would culminate in a *solution* to our marriage problems, not the end of our marriage. I was stunned that Jeremy had made up his mind so definitively.

One thing that sticks out in my mind during the tumultuous and confusing months following the Talk is how extraordinarily stressful it was to be out in public and attempt to put on a happy face. Fuuuck, it was excruciating. My homelife was falling apart—we hadn't told the kids or made anything official (we were in that bizarre limbo of trying to "figure things out")—and I had to go out and face people every day and pretend like I was just fine. All I wanted to do was become a hermit and hide from everyone, but life had to go on as usual for the kids. So I busted out my acting chops and tried to put on my best, hardest performance yet as a woman who was holding it together. I felt like a big, fake Stepford wife. I pleasantly answered when people asked, "How's Jeremy doing?" I made excuses for why he wasn't at school or community events. ("He's holed up watching the big game!" or "Oh, he just has a lot of work to do.") I became an unwilling expert at coming up with excuses on the fly. And it stressed me out. Why was *I* the one maintaining a public farce with the kids? I didn't want to be the rock. I wanted desperately to have the freedom to fall apart.

I held it together in public, but in front of my parents and brothers and just a few select, trustworthy friends, I did let myself fall apart. It felt like one big ball of unraveling shame. I first shared the news of my impending divorce with family members by email because I couldn't face anyone. It was somewhat impersonal, but it was the only way I knew how to explain my confusing and sorrowful feelings: through written words. They all offered immediate help and a shoulder to cry on. I still felt totally and utterly alone.

I felt like the only person who was going through this, and I don't mean that metaphorically, although I obviously wasn't the only one. But I *was* the only person I *personally* knew who was going through a divorce with kids. "Divorce" was not part of my vocabulary. I come from a long line of long-term marriages. My grandparents were married for seventy years at the time they passed away. My parents have been married for over fifty years. My brothers are still in marriages that have lasted fifteen and twenty-plus years. My neighborhood was full of happy, intact marriages and families. I was the black sheep. I had no frame of reference, and I was self-conscious about it and devastated.

I immediately went back on antidepressants and anti-anxiety meds. I felt like I was constantly stuck in survival mode. I started seeing my therapist again, practically begging on my knees for her to fix me and fix my marriage and explain how everything got to this desperate, horrific point. I became a robot, going through the motions of daily life and keeping the kids on their schedule, then falling to pieces and crying when I was alone.

It's agonizing to watch the man you married and vowed to spend the rest of your life with become a completely different person. I think divorce really brings out the worst in people, and I include myself in that statement. Going through our split, Jeremy, who is an attorney by trade, became Lawyer Ice Man. Everything that came out of his mouth was unrecognizable legalese. Lemme tell ya: Divorcing a lawyer is a special kind of hell. What happened to the loving husband I married? Here was this stone-faced, cold statue who only wanted to discuss divorce business and only when absolutely necessary. Forget talking about *feelings* or the last ten years of our relationship. We never really did that in a way that was satisfactory to me, which may have contributed to how long it took for me to feel any healing after the divorce.

I, on the other hand, became Raving Hysterical Female. For some reason, I felt that I could get him to change his mind by hurling as many insulting word vomits at him via text, using as many expletives and descriptive words as possible. (Weird how *that* method didn't work.) I just couldn't stop myself from pouring all of the sad, angry, confused thoughts in my head into emails. I'm sure Jeremy would be surprised to learn that, for as many emotional emails and texts I sent to him, I had an equal number of drafts that I *didn't* send. I coped by writing. A word of advice to anyone going through a divorce: Write more letters that you *don't* send than ones you do. I wish I had done this.

We were unrecognizable to each other. Neither of us looked anything like the people we had married ten years prior. It was a sad thing to witness, and even more devastating to experience firsthand.

I was desperate to keep the marriage together. Divorce was a foreign concept to me, and I'd never so much as imagined getting divorced. This was not part of my life plan. Divorce was something that happened to other people, not me! Most of all, I wanted to keep the family unit intact. This was the most critical thing to me. I wanted to keep the family together for the kids so they wouldn't have to grow up with split parents in two homes. I wanted them to grow up with an intact family unit, just like I had.

It was during one of our never-ending, circular arguments in which I was futilely trying to list all of the reasons he should stay that Jeremy abruptly interrupted and blurted, "I will not be held hostage by your mental illness any longer!" And there it was. With those twelve words I felt every ounce of the enormous burden I had placed on him.

Those words echoed in my head. "Held hostage." *Trapped.* Against one's will.

He didn't want to be here, but had felt unable to leave for who knows how long. He wanted to break free from the chains my mental illness had wrapped so tightly around his patience. He needed to escape. He needed to escape *me.*

So free he went. And I was left alone to pick up the pieces of my broken self, blaming myself for being so intolerable that I drove away the one person who had promised to love me forever, "in sickness and in health." *I guess I was too sick for even eternal vows*, I thought.

I have the glorious gift of perspective now, almost seven years later. I'm sure we would both have handled those conversations differently if we'd had perspective then.

The most important thing perspective has taught me, and what I want to tell anyone out there who has been made to feel too broken to love, is that *your illness does not define you.* It does not define your self-worth. And anyone who has made you feel otherwise—well dang it, that says a lot more about

One of my first headshots.

PHOTOGRAPHY BY JORJETTE

My first role, playing the baby Jesus, with my dad as Joseph and my mom as Mary.

Family photo, circa 1986. *From left:* brother Darin, Dad, Mom, me, and brother Justin.

Wayne Northrop ("Roman Brady") and I on the set of *Days of Our Lives* on my birthday, with the Barber pole cake!

Me and Candace, circa 1991.

With Jodie on the Sail With The Stars cruise.

A "school" field trip to the zoo.

Celebrating the final taping of *Full House* with John Stamos.

My boyfriend Ben and I with the cast right before our send-off to my prom.

You meet some of your best, lifelong friends in college. Greg is one of my favorites!

With my sorority sisters, the Palmers, at Whittier College. Yes, I'm wearing a cactus corsage, courtesy of my friend Greg.

Getting a taste of international travel at Oktoberfest in Germany, circa 1997.

My graduation from Whittier College, 1999. *From left:* Dad, Mom, grandmother Mary, me, brother Darin, sister-in-law Stephanie, grandfather Jim.

ROBERT EVANS

Jeremy and me on our wedding day.

First dance.

I couldn't have imagined my wedding day without Candace there.

ROBERT EVANS

It meant so much to me to have Jodie there on my wedding day.

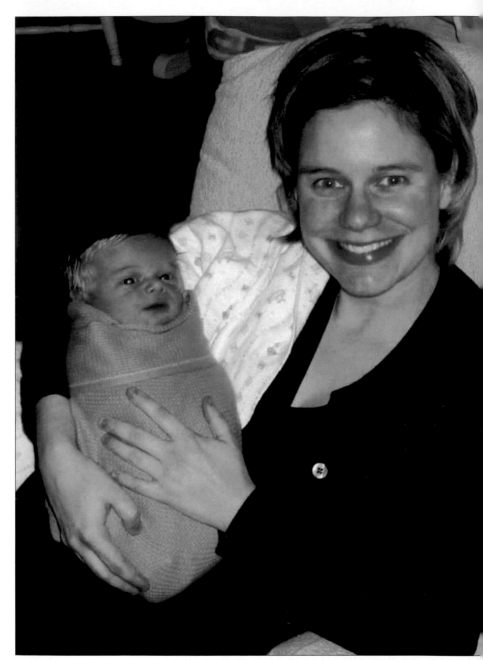

Baby Tate at one week old!

Family Christmas photo of 2007—the only shot where the kids were holding still...

One of the few photos I love of me (as a single mom),
with my kids and my dog, Holly. On vacation in Big Bear, 2016.

Completing the Hollywood Half Marathon, one of my 30-plus half marathons.

The She Wolf pack at my 4.0-mile 40th-birthday run, July 3, 2016.

Crossing the finish line of my first full marathon, Nike Women's Marathon in San Francisco.

Promoting season one of *Fuller House* with Jodie and Candace,
as they teach me how to work a press tour!

Jodie and I backstage with our girls, Felicity and Zoie,
who were extras on a season three episode.

I'M ON A BUS! A surreal moment while promoting season one in New York City.

Jodie, me, and Candace posing with our moms, who were extras in season four.

One of many full circle moments, posing on the Tanner family couch
with my mom and my daughter.

The Gibblers,
with Soni Bringas
and Juan Pablo
Di Pace.

Family photo
in the Tanner
convertible
while shooting
season three of
Fuller House—
also the 30th
anniversary of
Full House!

With Jodie, season one.

Doing press with Candace and Jodie the day after we taped the first episode of *Fuller House*. We had the fabulous Rennie Dyball as our interviewer—full circle moment indeed!

Jeff, Candace, and me at a Fourth of July party in Jeff Franklin's backyard.

My first date
with Michael.

With Felicity, Tate,
and Michael in 2018
at my mom's 75th
birthday celebration.

There's no place like home!

their (in)ability to cope with people with mental illness that it says about you.

You are more than your mental illness. *So much more.* Surround yourself with people who love you for you, broken parts and all.

The more stressful and upsetting the relationship became, the more miles I found myself running. The physical release was essential. But the mental release was just as critical. Writing was cathartic, but I needed a space where I could get away from anything divorce-related. Running fulfilled that. And so did something else—something unexpected.

The New Kids on the Block, or NKOTB, was my all-time favorite boy band when I was a teenager. I had the posters, the magazines, the shoelaces, and even the bedsheets. I was convinced that I was their #1 fan and that I was going to marry Joey McIntyre. (Ha! Get in line, sister.) My teenage daydreaming about Joey McIntyre is what got me through my awkward as hell middle school years. I used to imagine what it would feel like to actually be cool/pretty/charismatic/confident enough to be liked by a boy like Joey Mac. When I found myself overwhelmed with insecurity or embarrassment at not fitting in, these daydreams were like a buoy for me.

More than twenty years later, NKOTB came back into my life at a time when I needed them most. I can imagine the easy jokes to be made about the fact that a boy band was part of what helped me get through my divorce. But this was, in fact, the case.

The band had broken up in the '90s, but they reunited in

2008, to the delight of die-hard fans like myself. It's an ironic similarity to what my own life would become with the reboot of *Full House*. Right before shit started hitting the fan in my marriage, I had worked on an advertisement for NKOTB's summer Mixtape concert in Hershey, Pennsylvania. Their manager, Jared, invited me to be a guest at the concert festival weekend, and I couldn't pass it up.

By the time the show weekend rolled around that summer, though, I was thoroughly preoccupied with figuring out what the hell was happening with my quickly disintegrating marriage. I almost canceled the entire trip. But Jeremy encouraged me to go—I think as a way of getting some much-needed space away from me—and my dear friend and travel buddy Julie said it would be healthy for me to escape for a weekend. So off I went to the Mixtape festival weekend with Julie by my side.

I felt like a giddy teenager again without a care in the world. *MY GOD*, did I need that. I needed that feeling like I needed blood in my veins. It was a complete mental escape from my personal life. The songs brought back those feelings of being thirteen and carefree. Music is such a powerful link to our senses, and it can trigger such potent emotions. I felt pure joy and happiness. I felt a release. I felt free. I needed all of that even more than I realized at the time. I laughed and danced in the rain and sang at the top of my lungs, letting it all out. It filled my soul with a happiness I hadn't felt in a long time.

But when Julie and I boarded the plane to go home after the weekend, that sense of dread and depression came rushing back. I cried the entire flight home on her shoulder. I was desperate to hang on to the carefree fun I'd just had over the weekend. And I feared what was waiting for me back home.

Jeremy moved out of the house the next day. I was gutted, devastated, defeated.

I think a lot of people wonder why I have become so obsessed with NKOTB again as a full-grown woman. I've gone to a dozen of their concerts during the last several years, and I even went on several of their chartered cruises. I'm sure it seemed like I was having a midlife crisis or just desperately clinging to my youth. But NKOTB was my escape. It was my happy place at a difficult time when I didn't have many things to be happy about. So I clung to those giddy feelings like a life preserver. It would be silly to say I still have a crush on Joey. (The thought of him potentially reading that sentence makes my cheeks hot with embarrassment!) But it isn't a "crush" in the teenage sense; it's a nostalgic, sentimental appreciation for the hope he brought me at a time I really needed it. Joey serenaded me recently at Jeff Franklin's birthday party with "Please Don't Go Girl," a song that still makes me misty eyed. My heart swooned with love for all that he represented to me as a young girl, plus the realization that he is even more wonderful in person than I'd even imagined, all those decades ago.

It took a lot of time to heal from my divorce. A LOT of time. I think entire Alaskan glaciers moved in the time it took me to not feel completely broken every minute of the day. It also took a long time just for the process of divorce to even happen. I'm mostly to blame for that, because I desperately wanted to keep my divorce hush-hush—from everyone on earth, honestly, but particularly from the media. I'd been around long enough to see how these tabloid vultures get ahold of celebrity court documents and publish them very publicly and humiliatingly. So on top of all the painful feelings of going through a divorce, I had this added celebrity stress to contend with. Our lawyers took careful steps to figure out how to file everything as privately and confidentially as possible. Still, even with a prolonged divorce (thanks to the attorneys working at that same glacial speed), my unresolved grief outlasted everything else.

Grief is such a powerful, unpredictable emotion. It had power over me for a long time. It felt like my life was being dictated by my grief and mourning over the loss of my marriage. I kept feeling mad at myself. *Why can't I get over this? What is wrong with me?* I had to eventually learn that there is no time line for grief. You can't predict how long or how deeply you will grieve. There is no formula: "Divide the number of years of the relationship by half, and that is how long it takes you to recover." That equation is pure bullshit. You cannot arithmetic your way into healing. It takes as long as it's gonna take.

So I had to allow myself to feel how I felt. I didn't stuff my emotions away. If I felt sad, I FELT SAD. If I felt like crying, I CRIED HARD. And then (this was the critical part) I had to force myself to move on to something else for the rest of the day. I had to force myself not to dwell on my grief. I literally had to tell myself, "We are leaving the house, now!" and do anything—walk around the mall, call a friend for coffee, go see a movie. Movement and distraction were critical. Allowing myself the freedom to feel my emotions gave them validity.

But it was equally important for me not to dwell, ruminate, or spin. It took me a long time to learn this. I spent too long shaming myself by thinking, *I should be over this by now*. But I eventually realized: My grief is my own, and no one dictates how I feel or when I feel or how long I feel other than ME. So I owned it. *Felt* it. Only then was I able to release it.

I spent a long time being afraid of emotions that were difficult, emotions that raised my anxiety. Part of my growing anxiety was *fighting* the anxiety. My intense need to will the anxiety away simply heightened it. So I had to learn to sit with difficult emotions, sit with my Anxiety Beast right next to me on my couch. It was uncomfortable. I wanted to crawl out of my own skin. I bit my nails down. My stomach felt queasy, and my hands were jittery. But I forced myself to sit with these feelings to build a better tolerance for them, one big, deep breath at a time.

I had to learn to get comfortable with being uncomfortable, a skill I would hone over and over as a runner training for a marathon. The marathon doesn't ever *not* hurt. You just get better and better at tolerating pain. Eventually, I realized that it is in these moments of being comfortable with the uncomfortable that I found the most clarity.

My divorce eventually became final, but I never made an announcement. Even to this day, I have never formally or officially proclaimed, "I am divorced!" (Well, until now, I guess.) People eventually figured it out because I stopped mentioning Jeremy or posting pictures of him on Facebook. Family pictures had a noticeably absent father figure. It was just me and the kids. Just the three of us. This was our new normal.

There are one or two friends (in addition to my parents) who proved to be a lifeline during my divorce. And I can't overstate the importance of what they did for me, particularly in the times they just listened without judgment. One of these friends is Greg, from college and study abroad, who wrote me letters— pages and pages of handwritten letters!—during my divorce to remind me of my self-worth. He prompted me to allow myself to ugly cry and feel all the emotions in order to move on, and offered to sit beside me and hug me through it all. I still have those letters, that's how much they meant to me. (Greg knows that words are my love language!) I realize now how critical it is to find that one or two people with whom you can air your grievances and trust them to be a vault for your ugly emotions. These friends helped me become whole again.

My kids were great through the entire transition. It baffles me to this day how strong they were and still are. I still fear on a very deep level that the lasting effects of divorce will one day show up in them. But during the tumultuous period, they were like little champs. It certainly helped that Jeremy and I, for as much as we weren't getting along at the time, remained a solid parenting unit. The kids weren't stuck in World War III between Mom and Dad. Jeremy and I were always there for them, both when we were together and when we were apart. We went to parent-teacher conferences together. We showed up for school assemblies together. For a while, we still did family outings (dinners, birthday trips to Build-A-Bear) together. We weren't married to each other or living together anymore, but we tried really hard to keep our kids' family as intact as possible.

Let me stress: This was *not* easy. I had to swallow a certain amount of pride and hold my tongue frequently and put all of my personal feelings on hold for the moment. In essence, I had to eat the shit sandwich. The best advice I have for anyone else going through this with children is: Be kind to your former spouse in front of your kids, never say rude things about them in front of the kids; don't slander them in public; and finally, find that one trusted friend with whom you can let out all those feelings you've been bottling up.

I've been doing the co-parenting thing with my ex-husband for many years now, and it's still hard. But it has gotten easier as time passes. It's not a perfect system, by any means, and we still disagree on some parenting issues. The kids don't always want to stay at one or the other parent's house (depending on who they're annoyed with at the moment). They are always forgetting their homework/jackets/whatever at the other parent's house. The kids will also pit us against each other, saying, "But Dad always lets us do _____ at his house!" or "Mom said we could _____!" If one parent says "no" to a request, the kid will go to the other parent to get their "yes." Parenting is stressful, full stop. No matter what your situation is. Divorced families have unique challenges that may be similar or different to other families, and you just have to roll with it.

There is a saying: "The greatest gift a man can give his children is to love and respect their mother." (It applies equally to women showing respect to the children's father.) And although the sentiment originated with married people, I firmly believe it can hold true with divorced couples, too. You don't have to like or even care remotely about your ex-spouse. But treating them with respect and kindness (even if it's not necessarily deserved) goes a long way. And you know what? My kids deserve that much.

One image that is burned into my brain forever is the look my son had on his face the day his father and I told him we were getting a divorce. It was a look of shock mixed with hurt and the struggle to hold back tears . . . and it broke my heart into a million pieces. Here was the face I'd looked at every day of his life with an expression I'd never seen before. I will never forget that look. And I decided in that very moment that I would do anything and everything humanly possible to make life okay for my kids.

The first several times my son and daughter left for a weekend at their dad's house felt painfully bizarre to me. I didn't know what to do with myself. Even years later, I still feel that pang in my chest right after I kiss them goodbye and close the front door. There is a silence in my house that's deafening. I will clean my kids' rooms vigorously in an attempt to block out sad thoughts. And then I stop and allow myself to feel sad for a few moments. I think how, although it never gets easier, it does become more predictable.

I didn't realize it at first, but that kid-free breathing space was critical to my healing. I had the space to cry. I had the space to fall apart without the kids watching. I had the space to find out who I was again. Who was I? I was a thirty-six-year-old mom of two, but what else? What TV shows did I enjoy watching? Was I still a fan of books? What did I want to do in my spare time? I literally didn't know what to do with myself, after mothering and housekeeping and wife-ing and actively uncoupling over the past ten years.

I think, initially, I feared those kid-free weekends alone. I feared being by myself and, more specifically, the thoughts in my head that I wouldn't be able to escape. My depression was still pretty intense in those early years, and I was afraid of all the feelings that come along with loneliness.

I think loneliness—the word in general—conjures up negative emotions: sadness, fear, pity. But when I think back to my most recent years of being *alone*, I don't feel any of those things. In fact, I think those times of being alone, with just myself, were some of the most profound and informative times of my life. If anything, I *grew* from that period of solitude. Finally, I had the time and space to breathe. And think. And discover who I was again.

I took that time to simply sit with myself. *By* myself. I used the time to rediscover parts of myself that had been buried under my marriage for far too long. I mourned. I wept. I breathed deeply. I slept. I laughed. I found the things that made me smile again. Running. Binge-watching crime dramas. Reconnecting with friends I hadn't seen in years. Sleeping in. Journaling. Eating Chinese food on the couch. Reading biographies.

I finally rediscovered myself.

Here's the thing about loneliness and solitude: There's basically one main difference between them—fear. Loneliness is only lonely because of the *fear* that you will forever be alone. Solitude is simply the other side of the coin. It's being comfortable with the idea of being alone, without any fear.

Looking back at those fresh-single-mom years, I think I learned to embrace solitude. Not because I knew with any certainty I would be recoupled someday, but because I really *needed* it. Being comfortable with being alone reaps so many rewards. Once I let go of the fear that it would be forever, I could relax and settle into myself.

Solitude is really a rare and beautiful thing.

I also took this alone time to "unpack" my failed marriage and all of the emotions I had surrounding it. I needed to understand it in order to move on, but "understanding" it didn't simply mean cursing and laying all the blame on my ex-husband. In order to really and truly unpack this chapter of my life, I needed to understand my *own* role in the breakdown of the relationship. I needed to figure that out and own it. We both made mistakes, but rather than rehashing and reliving those mistakes continuously, I needed to recognize and fully accept the part I played in reaching this place in life.

It would be dishonest if I say I never thought about the role my anxiety played in the breakdown of my marriage. I wouldn't say it *caused* the breakdown, but it certainly contributed. Probably a lot. Do I feel bad about that? Absolutely. I beat myself up about it for a long time. I still think about it to this day. I know how difficult and exhausting it is to live with someone who suffers from anxiety; there are many days I wish I could escape *myself*. I wish I had gotten help earlier in my life and learned everything that I know now about my specific brand of anxiety. I wish I'd had the coping tools that I have now earlier in my marriage. Most of all, I wish Jeremy and I had gotten help together as a team and tackled my anxiety with proactive care and support.

Maybe I'm still unpacking that when I think about my anxiety in the context of my current relationships—with my children, my boyfriend, my work relationships, my friends. I can absolutely still be a crazy-maker to the people in my life. I know that and own it. I know that I overthink everything. I also know that when I overthink something, I want to talk about it over and over again, seeking a solution that I'll never find. I know that I have control issues. I know even in the heat of the moment that I shouldn't be controlling, but I do it anyway. I know that my anxiety sometimes presents itself in the form of anger and yelling. I know that my anxiety leads me to cancel plans or avoid phone calls. I know that my anxiety led me to believe for a long time that I could only earn the love of those around me by appeasing them. This is who I am. I have flaws, I acknowledge them, and I'm also always seeking to improve in those areas. Most importantly, I've learned this: Surrounding myself with people who accept me and all of my idiosyncrasies has been very healing. It's shown me that I am worthy of love and acceptance. I have people in my life who tell me, "I love you, even when your anxiety is at its worst, and we will get through this together." I cherish those people. I'm hanging on to them tight.

When it comes to divorce in general, I'll be the first to admit that I'm one of the very lucky ones. I got to keep my house, and I didn't have to downsize into an apartment. My kids didn't have to change schools. There were no abuse or addiction issues. I had a large support network. I had health care that includes mental health coverage. I acknowledge my enormous privilege and there's not a single day I take that for granted. I wish everyone going through a divorce could be as fortunate, because it was damn near excruciating to navigate even with all of my advantages. I would like to think that going through something so traumatic has made me a more empathetic person. I'm not so quick to judge people, because truly, you never know the struggles a person is facing.

But when I was in the thick of becoming a newly single mom, there was still a huge void that seemed impossible to fill, no matter how hard I worked or how little sleep I got. Even Super Single Mom did not equal Two Parents in One Home. It felt like a Herculean task to try to be *everything* to my kids (Mom, Dad, caretaker, cook, chauffeur, housekeeper, mentor).

Being a single mom comes with challenges I didn't anticipate, things I took completely for granted while living with a spouse. Like needing last-minute school project supplies thirty minutes before the store closes and having to haul both your children, who are already in pajamas, to the store because there isn't another adult in the house to watch them. I was also surprised at just how much I missed having another adult in the house to laugh with over the stories about the kids or relate to over the frustrations of parenting. There were many nights when I wanted so badly to share all of the funny things that Felicity said that day, but no one was there to listen or laugh with me. The isolation and loneliness of being a single mom can be crushing.

One of the most frustrating parts of the day-to-day of being a single mom was feeling the lack of help around running a household. All those things that Daddy used to do—kill all the spiders in the bathtubs, fix the leaky faucet, run out to the store late at night for toilet paper, help manage one kid's meltdown while the other kid was vomiting—all of those tasks were mine and mine alone now. And I thought motherhood was overwhelming *before* I got divorced! Even something as simple as taking out the trash on Sunday night turned into a minefield when I ran into a neighbor who innocently said to me, "Why are you taking those trash cans out by yourself? That's a husband's job!" *Welp, not anymore. It's just me.* This was a pretty sexist comment, too, which made me doubly uncomfortable. But it also highlighted my insecurities about being a single mother and how much I resented it.

I constantly felt inadequate as a single mom. I was never *enough*. I never had enough time to do things with the meticulous care I was used to. I never had enough hands to fill out all the forms and fold all the laundry and shop for all the groceries and pay all the bills. I was never patient enough with my kids. I never felt like I had enough energy to do all the things I needed to do. I wasn't strong enough to move Tate's bed when he wanted to rearrange his room. I didn't know enough about home maintenance to fix the toilet. I kept comparing myself as a single parent to the strength of a two-parent couple. And I continuously came out feeling inadequate. I resented Jeremy for putting me in this situation, I resented myself for failing to keep our marriage together, and I resented my anxiety for making everyday things seem infinitely more difficult. It was a dark, angry place to be, far away from a place of acceptance or healing.

My struggle with single motherhood is usually seasonal, meaning I'm triggered certain parts of the year. The holidays are definitely one of these triggers, and the first Christmas after my divorce was the hardest. I dreaded opening Christmas cards. I opened the first few holiday greetings with a lump in my throat and felt pang after pang of hurt at the images of smiling, happy families reminding me of what I once had and what was no longer in my life. And after diligently sending out our family Christmas card every year for almost a decade, I abruptly stopped. Silence. I didn't have any happy year-in-reviews to send out.

I stopped opening the holiday envelopes after a few days and put them aside to open later. The pile of envelopes grew taller and taller. Christmas came and went. And I never opened those cards. In a fit of post-holiday purging, I threw them all in the trash, unopened. I felt very ashamed about it and beat myself up for being selfish. But I just couldn't bring myself to open them and face those feelings.

Now I'm in a different place. With each holiday card I receive, I no longer see a reflection of what I've lost; I see a reflection of everything I've gained: all of the wonderful, beautiful, loving people in my life. It just reminds me of how very lucky I am.

Another sad milestone that I dreaded was putting up Christmas decorations in my house for the first time without a partner. I was not emotionally ready for the task, nor did I believe I was physically capable. I decided to tackle this monumental undertaking while the kids were at their dad's one weekend. I would save the ornaments and tree-trimming and fun stuff for the kids, but the nuts and bolts of Christmas needed to go up, and I wasn't sure exactly how I was going to do it.

I brought down every Christmas storage box in the garage. The ones that were too heavy for me to lift alone I managed to awkwardly bump down one step of the ladder at a time, sometimes just dropping the whole damn box on the floor.

I grunted and struggled and sweated and almost threw my back out trying to wrestle the tree into my living room, cursing my lack of upper-body strength out loud to my empty house. I hung each Christmas light by myself at the top of the ladder, knowing full well that if I fell, there was no one around to catch me (but at least I'd die doing something cheery!).

And you know what? After all the work was done and I wiped the dusty sweat from my brow, I looked around at my Christmas-filled house with awe.

I did that.

I. DID. THAT.

All of it.

It was the proudest moment I'd felt in my single life so far. Move over, pity party! Mom just slayed Christmas.

I knew in the back of my mind that I had more daunting tasks ahead of me. In a few weeks, I would also have to tackle my first Christmas alone with the kids, and then I would have to take all these damn decorations *down*. But for that moment? I basked in the pride of my self-reliance. Maybe I would survive this chapter after all.

In addition to all of the anxiety and difficulty swirling around the divorce, I had the added stress of my kids meeting their father's new girlfriend. Jeremy moved on after our marriage at the speed of light . . . or at least, that's how it felt to me. He moved on a lot faster than I did, and coping with that—both personally and helping my children adjust—was one of the most taxing parts of this already tumultuous period in my life. I saw her as The Enemy, someone else to blame for my anger and resentment. I saw Jeremy and Kelli not as two autonomous adults choosing to share their life together, but as insensitive, selfish people who were actively trying to make my life more difficult. I could not see past my anger. My kids enjoyed her company immensely, which felt like one, big, slap-in-the-face betrayal. Here I was, sobbing alone at night and trying to be single SuperMom . . . and they were off *bowling*? In what universe was this fair?

It took me a lot of time to accept their relationship. I'm not sure what exactly prompted the turning of the tide for me; maybe it really was just a case of "time heals all wounds." But the first Thanksgiving the kids spent with their dad, I found myself feeling gratitude. I wrote Kelli a note. This was the first time I would be meeting her in person, when I dropped the kids off at their dad's new apartment. I was nervous AF. But I decided that if there was ever a time to extend an olive branch, Thanksgiving was as good a time as any. I knew I wouldn't be able to eloquently say any of these things in person, so in the note I told Kelli that I was grateful for her positive presence in my kids' lives. My kids enjoyed being with her, and I appreciated her treating them so kindly. And I meant those things.

Jeremy and Kelli are married now, with an adorable three-year-old daughter. Each step was difficult for me, I admit—the engagement, their wedding, the pregnancy. But at some point, I stopped wishing that their relationship didn't exist and started feeling at peace with the fact that they made each other happy and, in turn, they treated me (and our kids) with so much kindness. They allowed me the space to be angry and process. Jeremy gave me a courtesy heads-up whenever they hit a milestone that he knew I would need time to process and wouldn't want to hear about from other people. Kelli has been nothing but gracious and a wonderful example of how a step-mom should be. It took a long time to get here, but I can honestly say now that I am grateful to Jeremy and Kelli for their grace and kindness and for always putting our kids first.

It's been seven years since that fateful Talk. During all the suffering I went through as my marriage was falling apart, and through the subsequent divorce, I would never have believed that I'd get to the healthy place I'm in today. That day of the Talk signifies a lot. It's no longer the worst day of my life. It's now the day I survived—the first day I began to endure and persevere.

Jeremy and I have a cordial, friendly relationship now. I continue to appreciate his wife for the love and care she gives my children. We all co-parent openly and honestly and proactively. Some might say our relationship is a little *too* cordial, and it's definitely not typical of divorced parents. We have keys to each other's houses. We sit next to each other at soccer games and chat. My boyfriend, Michael, and I attended the first birthday party of Jeremy and Kelli's little girl, my kids' sister, Abbey. My children seem unaware that our way of functioning together is not typical. This was most evident when Felicity asked recently why Jeremy wasn't going on the Barber Family Disney Cruise with my entire side of the family. She was legitimately perplexed as to why he wasn't coming.

I don't know exactly when we ended up in this place, but I'm grateful that we did. Once each side started showing the other grace, things turned. We let go of the little things . . . perhaps the big things, too. It's not worth it to me anymore to get angry; it's too much damn effort, and I'm tired!

Regardless, we are in a good place. It helps (me) to think of Jeremy and Kelli not as "that married couple that we no longer are" but as a loving dad and stepmom to Tate and Felicity. I think of Abbey as their sister, whom they love so much. There are times when Felicity is still confused. One day she asked "Is Abbey my stepsister or my half sister? What's the difference?" I replied, "She is your *sister*. We don't love in halves, we love with the whole of our hearts."

Love and kindness are reciprocal when you allow them to be . . . and when you do, everyone wins.

As for my own love life after divorce, I couldn't even think about dating for a very long time. I was still adjusting to my new normal. I needed more time to process the past ten years of my life. I felt like I still had lessons to learn. I didn't want to repeat the same mistakes. I couldn't imagine I'd ever reach the point of thinking, "I'm ready to date again." I didn't even know *how* to date! When Jeremy and I first met, there was no Tinder or eharmony. How do you even meet people these days? Dating after a decade of being married was totally out of my comfort zone. I had the added benefits of being socially anxious *and* a celebrity. Where was *that* how-to manual?

Perhaps one of the most important lessons I learned from my divorce came out of a therapy session when I was feeling especially insecure. My therapist asked me about the character I played for eight years in front of millions of people.

˙"You know that character?" My therapist looked me in the eye. "The one with the unshakable confidence? There is a piece of her inside of you."

I remained skeptical.

"But I was just acting," I argued. My therapist shook her head.

"No. That confidence and love for life is deep inside of you. Otherwise, you would never be able to play her."

Game changer. I was stronger than I ever knew.

When I met (my now boyfriend) Michael at a half marathon in Los Angeles and he asked me out on a date, I didn't even recognize it as being asked out on a date. I thought he was inviting me along on a group lunch, which is the only reason I agreed. When I finally realized he meant a real date, I panicked and said, "No. I'm not dating. Maybe ever again."

He was cool and patient, and we kept in touch via texting. After a few months, I realized that I really did like this guy. I agreed to go to dinner with him, but I insisted it was *just* dinner, and not a date. And that's how I adjusted to dating again—by being in denial. I guess as long as we weren't labeling it "dating" or using terms like "boyfriend," I was okay with it. I loved spending time with him and getting to know him. It took me probably six months of this unlabeled dating before I actually used the term "boyfriend." What can I say? I need a lot of time to adjust to something new.

I kept my relationship with Michael a secret for several months, just so I could figure out how I felt about him without other people's opinions clouding my own. It was a blissful season filled with all the butterflies and excitement of flirting and getting to know a person without the pressure of labels. I confessed to my therapist that I'd found someone special, but I wasn't sure I wanted to commit to someone again so soon ("soon" for me being defined as almost three years post-divorce!). She told me to stop overthinking everything, to relax and simply *enjoy* these feelings without fearing what would happen in the future.

Michael and I saw each other every day over the four days of winter break when my kids were with their father (as I've admitted, a difficult time for me). We went for a run together to the beach at sunset and had dinner and cocktails overlooking the ocean. We shopped at lululemon. We walked the Third Street Promenade in Santa Monica and shared coffee while people-watching. It felt so foreign to me—this "dating." Enjoying another adult's company and not worrying about my children. It was odd, but also freeing. And, to be honest, a little melancholy. I was transitioning to a new phase of my life. I said goodbye to Michael at the end of our four-day date, and we took a picture atop a parking garage. (My friend Julie later said she loved the way his finger caressed my hand in the picture, that it was very telling.) And as I made the hour-long drive back to my house, I cried. I cried for the multitude of emotions I was experiencing at once. I wasn't sure if my heart and head were ready to move on, but I felt a lightness I hadn't felt in a very long time. I felt joy. I was closing one chapter of my life and opening another. The tears flowed as I thought, *What an amazing thing to find your person after coming out of the depths of heartbreak.*

When Michael and I finally went public with our relationship, I soon discovered that people are nosy no matter what your marital status and want to know all about your business once you start dating again after your divorce. This made me annoyed and self-conscious; I was already a private person. It was hard to simply "enjoy the ride" when people kept prying into our business.

I'm still happiest just keeping things simple. I don't plan to get remarried. I don't feel the need to, and I don't think I want to go down that road again. But everyone seems to want to know if we are going to get married. Societal pressure to marry is seriously nuts. It's like people can't comprehend two people just simply *being together* and being happy with that. Reflecting after my divorce from Jeremy, I realized that my own personal motivation for getting married was so that I could have a family. I was very traditional in that way: You get married, you have children, you stay married forever. Without that intact family unit, I have a lot less motivation to get married again. But that doesn't mean I don't have the desire to spend my life with someone. I just don't want or need a label or a license. Michael and I recently went out to our favorite Italian restaurant to celebrate four years of being together. I posted a picture on Facebook, and everyone started chiming in with "Happy Anniversary!" replies. I admit, this felt very weird. I didn't think of it as a traditional "anniversary." It's just four years. With my person. Whom I love. It really is that simple.

CHAPTER TEN

Running for My Life

I AM NOT AN ATHLETE. I AM NOT AN ATHLETE. I repeat: I am *not* an athlete.

I think it's a common misconception that people who are athletically inclined were born that way. I'm here to tell you the opposite. I don't like sports. I actively hate football. Gyms make me visibly distressed.

But I do like to run. And that makes me a runner.

It wasn't always this way. I never played sports growing up. "Acting" was my after-school sport. P.E. was a chore, and I was notably relieved when I was working on Fridays and could skip the dreaded "mile" test.

I did not (and still don't) have an athletic build. I was always lanky and awkward; muscles weren't something I appeared to have in my body. My mom signed me up for tennis lessons one summer in an attempt to instill a sense of fitness in me, but this lesson became not only a sad display of my lack of fitness, but also my lack of coordination. Double bonus!

Sports just weren't *me*.

Fast-forward to college, where I decided I was going to be on the women's lacrosse team. Why? I don't really know. It seemed like a cool thing to do. Those lacrosse gals seemed like badass chicks, and I wanted to feel as strong as they appeared. Plus, I had a couple of friends on the team and, as you may have already gathered, I am easily persuaded by friends. So I ran out and bought all the equipment. I was fascinated by the lacrosse stick—what an unusual and curious apparatus! I lived on the West Coast, where lacrosse teams weren't as prevalent as on the East Coast, which made the sport seem even cooler. I was ready to *be. an. athlete!*

I showed up for the first lacrosse practice on a cold Tuesday evening. I was pumped. Here we go! The coach announced that we were going to warm up with a two-mile run.

Blink. Excuse me?

The two-mile run was just the *warm-up*? Shit.

With panic surging through my veins, I ran the most painful twenty minutes of my life. I trailed behind the rest of the team, but somehow finished. When I was done, I did not collapse (yay!) but I did throw up (boo). And then promptly walked over to the coach to tell her I quit.

My entire lacrosse career began and ended in less than thirty minutes—just about the length of a sitcom episode.

I accepted what I believed to be indisputable. I was not, and never would be, an athletic person.

In 2012, Disney hosted their inaugural half marathon in and around the Disneyland theme park and the streets of Anaheim, California. The race would be geared toward women and was named after Disney's beloved pixie with (fittingly) the ability to fly: Tinker Bell.

My friends were *all over this* and signed up on the first day of registration. They encouraged me to do the same, but I was not so easily convinced. I was intrigued, but *never* had I thought I could run thirteen miles. Me? The non-athlete? NO WAY.

Despite my self-doubt, I was curious enough to check out Disney's Tinker Bell Half Marathon website. The first thing I saw at the very top of the web page in big, red, bold lettering: "RACE IS 94 PERCENT FULL."

What?! *The race is 94 percent full? I can't miss out!* FOMO was in full effect. That's all it took. This clearly illustrates the power of persuasive marketing—I will sign up for just about *anything* if it's at 94 percent capacity. Root canals, colonoscopies, tax seminars, half marathons: Where do I sign up? What can I say?—I'm a sucker.

The thought of running thirteen miles really terrified me. As a response to this fear, I trained really hard. I didn't follow a specific training program, but I had gleaned from friends that I needed to be completing shorter runs (three to five miles) during the week and longer runs (seven to ten miles) on the weekends, gradually building up my mileage as the weeks progressed.

I had some difficulty: The first time I finished nine miles, I did NOT experience that infamous "runner's high"—rather, I wanted to kill someone and then amputate my legs. The best training advice I got was to "listen to your body" and back off the higher mileage if my legs were screaming (which they were). So I looked for other ways to push myself. In fact, some of my best training took place on a single hill near my house. I would run up the hill, then walk down, run up again and walk back down, and repeat that five times. It wasn't very long, distance-wise, but it really strengthened my legs.

When the Tinker Bell Half Marathon race day arrived, my goal, first and foremost, was simply to finish. The race rules stated that you had to finish the race in three hours, thirty minutes, or you would be "orange-flagged" and picked up in the Cart of Shame (not its official name) to be whisked to the finish line. The fear of this alone was enough to make me run faster. But based on my training, I was hoping to finish in three hours. Still, I had never actually run thirteen miles all in one go, so I really had no idea how my body would react.

My friends and I selected special outfits to wear on race day that included glittery makeup, tulle skirts, large fairy wings, and custom tank tops embroidered with "It's not sweat, it's pixie dust!" (Because it's all about dressing up, right?)

We started the race with some light jogging—there were a lot of bodies out there. Before I knew it, though, my friends started running like bats out of hell. As soon as there was even an inch of clearing in the sea of humanity, they were gone. And we were still on the first mile. Whoa, wait a minute, who *are* you people? We even ran through the first few water stations, which means we were running while trying to guzzle water. That's when I realized I might actually be running with crazy people. (Or professional athletes disguised as suburban moms.) Hello, adrenaline! That was the *only* thing carrying me through to keep up with my friends. Needless to say, those first two miles were painful.

One of the most difficult parts of trying to keep up with

these rabid pacemakers was navigating my way through the slower runners: *Oh, there's a space! Oh wait, that space is gone. Can I really squeeze through there? Oh, what the hell.* I definitely whacked no fewer than a dozen people with my wings, just trying to keep my team in sight. (I do feel bad about that.) Fortunately, my friends tempered their expressway pace by mile five or so, after which we were able to run at a much more reasonable speed.

Two miles of the course actually took us through Disney-land itself, which was such a highlight of the day. We ran through some of the backstage areas, usually only accessible to Disney cast members, and saw parade floats and Disney char-acters. We even spotted the Lost Boys riding the carousel! I an-ticipated seeing runners taking pictures with the characters, but I didn't anticipate runners stopping and *standing in long lines* to take pictures with the characters. (What about the Cart of Shame, people? Snap a quick pic and GO!) Anyhoo, run-ning down Main Street was a trip. The sun had just started to rise, the Sleeping Beauty Castle was in front of us, and the morning had an air of magic.

One of the best parts of the race was all the spectators cheer-ing for us runners and seeing all of the creative, handmade signs they waved to encourage us. Most were inspirational, like, "Don't give up! Remember all the reasons why you're running!" But some were just hilarious, like, "Making this sign took a lot of energy, too," and "Worst parade ever." We took pictures with our personal faves.

By mile nine, I was really starting to feel the pain. We had only stopped running once for a quick potty break and walked for a minute or two through the water stations. Aside from that, we had been running the whole way. It was just unreal—I had never run for this long without taking longer walking breaks. I never thought I could physically do this.

At the mile nine marker, the race had set up an energy gel station, so we grabbed our GU and sucked it down. I took this chance to quickly check my phone and read some of the messages people had sent me. I had eighty-two notifications! I was overwhelmed. The combination of GU and feeling all the love from friends gave me a huge surge of energy. I honestly felt better during miles nine through twelve than I did throughout any other part of the race. Never would I have anticipated this kind of lunacy!

At one point I even passed my friends and said, "I found my second wind . . . I'm just going to keep riding it!" We each seemed to experience our highs and lows at different points of the race, which was actually a good thing. When I was dragging and hurting, their determination pulled me through, and vice versa. We were inspired to keep going and to go faster by whoever was having their second wind at the time. Teamwork, baby!

At mile thirteen, we rounded the final bend from the virtually empty backlot of California Adventure and out onto Disneyland Drive, where there were suddenly *hundreds* of people—fans, family, spectators, photographers snapping pictures. It was a surreal moment, and suddenly I realized we were in the final tenth of a mile of this race. I looked at my friend Laurie and shouted, "This is it! We're in the homestretch!" I fought back tears as Revive's song "Blink" started playing on my iPod—the song that had played at my grandmother's funeral just a few weeks prior to this race. Everything came together in that single moment as I thought about everything that mattered most in my life: My family. My kids. My friends. The people without whom I never would have pushed myself or believed that I could conquer 13.1 miles. It was a glorious moment, nothing short of amazing. "Runner's high" does not even begin to scratch the surface.

Lily, Laurie, and I grabbed each other's hands, and with our arms stretched up over our heads, we crossed that finish line, two hours and forty-two minutes after we started.

At the risk of sounding melodramatic, this truly was a transformative experience. It's hard to put into words; something *changed* in me out there on that course. To actually accomplish something you never thought you could do, *and* set a personal record, *and* create incredible memories with dear friends, *and* run through the Disneyland castle while the sun is rising behind you . . . well, all of that was pretty darn miraculous.

I guess it's *not* all about the glitter and tulle, after all.

It was right about the time that I was finding joy in running that my marriage was falling apart. I didn't realize it in the moment, but running was about to become my best therapy to help me through the hardest period of my life. After the Tinker Bell race, I was hooked on running and immediately signed up for two more half marathons. These races took place just a few months before the Talk; I firmly believe now that God or some higher being was laying the groundwork for me to use running as an outlet for coping with the shit storm that was brewing.

In the months following the Talk, my anxiety and depression ramped up to high. I was robotic and running on autopilot, a shell of my former self. It took all my strength just to get through the day without falling apart in front of everyone. Running became my lifeline. I *needed* those endorphins as much as I needed oxygen. I ran to empty my brain of all the constant negative self-talk. I ran to distract myself from the drama taking place in my personal life. I ran to feel like someone other than "Mom" or "Soon-to-be-Divorcée," even if it was only for a few fleeting hours each week.

I was initially drawn to running because I could do it by myself. I don't have to talk to anyone, and I don't have to listen, which is soothing for an introvert and actually one of the ways we recharge our batteries. That silent part of my day is an essential piece of my mental well-being. But I have also come to appreciate the therapeutic aspects of *social* running. My friend April and I trained for a half marathon together, which meant hours of running side by side. Something happens when you run with another person; you find yourself opening up in ways that just don't happen with other forms of socializing or group exercise. It's a simultaneous physical and emotional catharsis that I've never experienced elsewhere.

Often, April and I were too winded to speak and run at the same time, but the conversations that did flow were so open and honest. Topics that would normally be difficult to talk about found their way into our conversations with refreshing transparency. The running seemed to bring dormant emotions up to the surface. April had also been a single mom with three kids for many years—not because of divorce, but because she was suddenly widowed. Although our circumstances differed, we found many of our challenges to be the same. She shared details surrounding the death of her first husband and finding her way as a single mom before eventually finding love again and marrying her high school sweetheart, Tim. She reminded me that happy endings can be born out of the darkest of circumstances. Similarly, I shared feelings about my grief and divorce that I hadn't ever been able to articulate before. The urge to communicate about this with her felt overwhelming, as if my words had suddenly gained momentum and couldn't wait to come out. The running was strengthening our bodies, yes, but we didn't expect that it would also strengthen our bond as friends and confidants. We hurt, we cried, we healed. Together.

The competitive aspect of sports has always made me uncomfortable, which is probably why I never followed through with lacrosse or any other team sport. But when I'm running, I'm competing against myself in an effort to better myself. I'm much more interested in reaching my own goals than beating someone else. Even if I don't best my finish time (and I usually don't), I usually do make some sort of significant discovery about myself during a run. That, to me, is a win.

I've noticed a surge of fitness movements that are about wanting to prove you're the toughest, the hardest, the most badass. These have never appealed to me—partly because they're intimidating, and partly because I don't need to feel like the toughest, hardest, most badass worker-outer. I don't want to kill my body. I just want to be *good enough* and incorporate some kind of movement (preferably running, sometimes something else, like barre) into my everyday routine. That's all I need.

And I wonder if there are others out there who, like me, didn't work out or do anything physical for years because they felt they weren't good enough. I wonder if more people would be motivated to get up and simply move their bodies if they didn't feel like they have to be some super-fit badass, but were just encouraged to exercise to feel better emotionally. I wish there was some sort of "It's Okay to Be Average!" movement.

Have you ever noticed how only the "fast" runners post pictures of their watches? Let's stop that. Let's stop that right now! I would like to start a revolution of "slow" runner brags. Calling all twelve-minute milers: I want to see *your* watch. I want all of us to "embrace the pace" and be proud of posting pictures of our stats. I want everyone to encourage everyone else. Because honestly, what's slow for one runner may be really fast for another runner. Speed is relative. But what unites us as runners is our love of the sport and the desire to better ourselves.

Roughly two years after this average runner began her love affair with running came the day I signed up to run a *full* marathon—an intimidating 26.2 miles.

This surprised everyone, even me. "Are you crazy?" nonrunner friends would ask. I gave a myriad of answers at the time: Peer pressure. It's on my bucket list. Temporary insanity.

But here is the truth: Earlier on the day that I registered for the marathon, I had signed the legal agreement that would signify the official end of my decade-long marriage. A few hours after the ink on my divorce papers was dry, I saw an announcement that Nike had opened its lottery registration for the Nike Women's Marathon in San Francisco—a race that was very hard to get into. And something just clicked. I knew I *had* to run the full marathon. It was an intense, visceral, inexplicable reaction to getting a divorce: Go run a marathon.

I registered for the lottery, and a month later I was notified that my name had been drawn. *I was going to run the marathon.* And suddenly, out of the hardest year of my life—one filled with all the immeasurable grief and pain that accompanies an unwanted and unexpected divorce—was born a unique opportunity that would signify strength, resilience, and self-growth.

I was ready to go.

The training was hard, even harder than I imagined it would be. I had many angry runs where I would pound out my anger with every slam of my foot into the pavement.

I had many runs where I felt like I wasn't doing enough.

I had some runs where I would put on my sunglasses and hat and just run and cry, embracing the physical and emotional release.

I had a few runs that I skipped entirely because I was too depressed to get out of bed.

There was one run that I did not actually *run*, but instead walked the entire eight miles because I was nauseated and a little dizzy from adjusting to a new anxiety medication. But I still got it done, one slow step at a time.

I also spent a lot of time alone out there on the road, doing eighteen-mile training runs by myself. I learned to embrace that solitude, just as I'd done on the couch on those first weekends when my children went to their father's, to use that alone time to pound everything out through the pavement. Adrenaline, muscle fatigue, endorphins, physical pain, emotional pain, baggage—it *all* came out through my feet.

And there were so many runs that made me feel strong. Runs that made me feel I was getting even stronger. Runs that, at the end, convinced me that I could face even the hardest challenges.

Running is as much about the mental aspect as it is the physical (if not more so). I trained my brain to help me overcome the physical strain of running 26.2 miles, and without realizing it until the end, I trained myself to overcome emotional suffering, too. I learned to accept and even lean into the suffering. As Thich Nhat Hanh says in *How to Fight*, "To try to run away from suffering is not wise. To stay with it, to look deeply into it, and to make good use of it, is what we should do. It is by looking deeply into the nature of suffering that we discover the path of transformation and healing." How did I make good use of all of that emotional pain? I turned it into a marathon.

At first, I thought this training was like some deep metaphor for how I was running away from all of my problems. But one day I realized, no, that's not it at all. That's totally the wrong metaphor. I wasn't running away from anything; in fact, I *found* myself out on those roads.

I was ready to take on 26.2.

I arrived at the start line of the Nike Women's Marathon in San Francisco, approximately twenty weeks after I had signed those divorce papers and registered for the race. I thought about how I got there, quite literally by putting one foot in front of the other. I realized running had become a metaphor for my post-divorce life. *Just keep moving, no matter how much it hurts.* My thoughts quickly dissipated as the starting gun went off and my body fell into the rhythm it had been preparing for all these months. I think I smiled for the entire first five miles.

When the marathoners split off from the half marathoners, right around mile eleven, we entered Golden Gate Park, which had almost a mythical, ethereal quality to it. It was misty and quiet, the road had been shut down to traffic, and there were only a few of us marathoners chugging along through the park. I could only hear the sounds of our breathing, our feet hitting the pavement, and the birds chirping above us. It was transcendent.

By the time we exited the park and started the long, final eight miles of the marathon along the Great Highway (which ironically didn't feel great at all in the moment), my running euphoria had been replaced by fatigue and soreness. Plus, it was freezing out there.

Let me tell you, it was the oddest sensation ever to have puffy hands that were freezing. My hands always swell when I run, and I usually attribute that to heat. But swollen *and* frozen? I imagined this is what cadavers must feel like—you know, if they weren't dead, and still had the ability to feel. It's like my limbs had just given up and *died*. Even blood flow was too taxing out there on the (Not-So) Great Highway.

It was right about then that I hit the infamous "wall" in the marathon. For anyone who has ever wondered what the wall feels like, I can only say this: Every expletive I had ever learned since junior high and new expletives that I was creating right there on the spot were all running through my mind, ready to explode out of my mouth at any moment. I was experiencing active rage at whoever designed this course and decided to f*ck up the mileage and make these last mile markers literally farther apart than the former miles. It was the part of the course that *would never end*.

At the turnaround at Lake Merced, there was a jumbotron set up with a livestream of runners. I guess this was meant to be a boost to us fatigued marathoners, but all I remember seeing was looks of despair on everyone's faces, like some bizarre death march.

I had been vacillating for the full twenty-two miles about whether or not to stop to use a porta-potty. I actually ran past the porta potties by a couple of yards, then turned back to use one. At this point, the pain in my legs was so intense, and I didn't need bladder pain on top of that. So I stopped. I thought I only spent a minute in the porta potty, but looking at the split later on? Holy cow, I was in there for three minutes. People: *All I did was pee*. That means it took me a full three minutes just to sit down and get myself back up. I knew I was struggling with the pain and my legs were shaking pretty hard, but I didn't realize I was in there for so long.

I finally crossed the 40K timing mat. Instead of relief, I felt irritation. 40K? What the hell is that? I'm an American, dammit, and I can't do metric math. Particularly with this marathon-induced brain fatigue. You expect me to do *multi-*

plication? Just tell me how many more steps I have to endure, fercryingoutloud!

The last mile of a marathon is surreal. The pain doesn't go away, and still, even with only a mile left, you wonder, *Will I be able to finish this race?* Suddenly, I started to see coaches lined on both sides of the street. (They are designated by their bibs, which read "COACH" instead of listing a number.) There were what seemed like hundreds of them, lined along the entire last mile. Some of them were running back to retrieve runners farther behind on the course. ZOMG! I panicked for two seconds, wondering if someone was going to approach me. Secretly, I was hoping not because I did *not* want anyone in my personal space at that moment. Don't you *dare* get near me, or I will somehow muster up what little strength I have left to bodycheck you. I needed a wide berth! I quickly realized that these coaches were there to support the purple Team In Training runners who were running on behalf of the Leukemia & Lymphoma Society. Whew! When they spotted a purple shirt, a coach immediately started pacing them and giving a pep talk. Even though this was not for me, I have to admit it was really inspiring to see. Someone was there—running, pacing, motivating, helping, encouraging—for no other purpose than to motivate a runner all the way to the finish line. Suddenly, I felt the surge I needed.

And finally, at last . . . I could see the finish line. For the first time in hours, I was no longer thinking about how much I hurt. All I could see was the word FINISH and the Nike swoosh. I started running as fast as I could, which felt like I was sprinting (even though I'm sure I was going at a turtle's pace). Suddenly, I heard my name. My friends Cathie and Eileen, who had finished the half marathon a few hours ago, were there to cheer me to the finish.

This was it! With relief, joy, utter exhaustion, and the stinging of hot tears in my eyes, I approached the final timing mat and the elusive finish line.

I crossed it five hours and forty-nine seconds after I started. I was holding back the tears, in shock that I could actually stop running now. Really? I can stop? That thought exhilarated me. I didn't have to run *ever again* if I didn't want to! It was surreal.

I heard my name again and looked to my right. I saw my good friend Lindsey and her husband Rob standing just beyond the finish line with the spectators. I didn't even know she was going to be there, and the tears kept flowing. By the time I reached Lindsey and Rob, I was in full-on ugly-cry mode. Lindsey hugged me, and I cried big, heaving, audible, uncontrollable sobs. And when I say uncontrollable, I literally mean that I physically could not stop crying. They were deep, guttural tears of joy, tears of relief, tears of exhaustion. I was so happy and so tired. The intensity of the pain in my body couldn't match the intensity of pride and sheer elation I felt inside of me. And I released it *all*. Everything that I had been holding in for so long came out through my tears.

I was shocked when I spoke and found that my voice was hoarse, as if I'd been screaming for the last five hours instead of running. After a few minutes, Lindsey pointed and said, "I do believe you have a nice piece of jewelry waiting for you over there." I hobbled down to the finisher's chute, where a volunteer scanned my bib, and on the other side were hundreds of firefighters dressed in tuxedos, carrying silver platters bearing little blue Tiffany boxes. At last, the highly anticipated moment had arrived. This finisher's chute was like the red carpet of marathons. I was presented with my Tiffany finisher's necklace and posed for a picture with a man in a tuxedo.

I *DID* IT!

I kept crying—not for the things I had lost, but for everything I had gained.

"That's the thing about running: Your greatest runs are rarely measured by racing success. They are moments in time when running allows you to see how wonderful your life is." This quote by elite marathoner Kara Goucher summed it up perfectly. In that moment, after the most painful year of my life, I felt nothing but all of the wonderfulness of everything I had to live for. All of the people who love me unconditionally. All of the lessons that made me stronger. All of the experiences that make life beautiful. *I felt like a champion.*

This marathon and my training taught me a lot. It helped me become more comfortable with things that make me uncomfortable. (Namely, pain.) It helped me realize the difference between fearing loneliness and embracing solitude. It helped me find an inner strength I didn't know I possessed. It allowed me to quiet the noise and focus. It helped me contemplate and accept the unexpected change in my life's new trajectory. It helped me understand that I can't always change my life's circumstances. *But I can change myself.*

The marathon taught me that the race is not even really about running. It's about the ability to endure. It's about the ability to keep moving forward, no matter how much it hurts. And most importantly, it's about believing. Believing that you can do it. So that's what I did. I endured, I kept moving forward, and I believed in my ability to do it. And that's what I will continue to do, in running and in life.

They say you lose yourself in the things you love. Sometimes, you find yourself, too.

CHAPTER ELEVEN

Returning to Hollywood

I CAN TELL YOU THE EXACT MOMENT my life changed.

It was Father's Day, 2013. Just four days prior, I had signed the official dissolution agreement that would eventually be filed with the courts to end my marriage. I was in a bad place, emotionally, mentally, physically. I didn't know how to pick up the pieces of my new single-mom life and move forward into what felt like a bleak future.

And then my phone rang. I looked down at the caller ID and saw Jeff Franklin's name.

That's odd, I thought. He rarely calls me.

Deep down, something flickered inside my core. Hope? Curiosity? I don't know what you'd call it. But it was a flicker I hadn't felt for a very long time.

Inside, I think I knew—maybe just wished?—that my life was about to change forever. And it did. I answered the call.

"How are you, and would you be interested in reprising your role as Kimmy Gibbler on a *Full House* spin-off?" was basically how Jeff greeted me. No small talk or beating around the bush—we had a show to make!

On that very brief first phone call, I didn't hesitate for even a moment. My answer was an unequivocal YES.

My knee-jerk response surprised even me. I had never had a desire to return to acting before, but to play a character again who I knew and loved, alongside people I grew up with and considered part of my family? Absolutely!

But first, we needed to sell the idea of the show to a network. The premise of *Fuller House* is a flip of the original series: Instead of three men raising three girls, three women would now be raising three boys and a girl. Like Danny Tanner in the original show, D.J. finds herself widowed and enlists the help of her sister and best friend to help her raise her boys in the original Tanner family home in San Francisco. Instead of being the kids on the show, Candace, Jodie, and I would now be the lead adults in a very full-circle fashion. The three of us joined Jeff and executive producer Bob Boyett to discuss the show's premise and a plan for pitching the show to networks.

We confidently assumed this would be easy. The original show, *Full House*, had been such a beloved hit during the '80s and '90s, and we had a solid base of loyal fans who still watched the series almost thirty years after it first premiered. This was a no-brainer, right?

Not so fast! The executives at the networks weren't as easily sold on the idea as we all were. Bob and Jeff were pitching the idea very well, and Candace, Jodie, and I were present for every meeting to show the executives in person that our chemistry as a cast was alive and well, but for whatever reason, there was a big disconnect. We received rejection after rejection. The networks just weren't sure that a "reboot" could be wildly successful. (This is ironic now, considering how many reboots have been developed since *Fuller House* premiered!)

There was a long stretch of time when I really thought the show would never be made. It was so disheartening, knowing how much the cast wanted to reunite for a spin-off and recapture that magic on set, and knowing just how happy it would have made all of our die-hard fans who still watched reruns of the original. I couldn't believe this wasn't a slam dunk, and worse, that it might never happen.

And then, one day, we got a call from Netflix. They had recently started developing their own original series, and they wanted to create original kids' and family-oriented programming. Well, how about that? Netflix was looking for a family show, and here we were looking to pitch a spin-off of the ultimate family show! Talk about a perfect relationship.

It took several more months to seal the deal, but I remember sitting in my car in the parking lot of a Starbucks with my venti peach iced tea one afternoon in April 2015 when Jeff called again, this time with the news that it was official: *Fuller House* was going to happen. I closed my eyes and smiled, secretly bursting inside, feeling relief and happiness and excitement. This was really happening!

We were still under a gag order and weren't allowed to talk about it with anyone until the official announcement was made. This became very difficult very quickly, as rumors surrounding the spin-off were spreading, and all of my friends were asking me, "Is *Full House* coming back?"

I had to get very creative with my answers. "That's been a rumor for years!" I would reply, which technically wasn't a lie. Then I would quickly change the subject.

On April 21, 2015, it was finally, officially announced: The *Full House* sequel, *Fuller House*, would be premiering on Netflix in 2016. I made my own little announcement on my Instagram by posting a picture of my old *Full House* director's chair (which I'd kept all these years!) with a script and a pair of rainbow tights, alongside the caption: "WE'RE BACK! After almost 20 years . . . my bright tights are officially coming out of retirement. The *Full House* sequel #FullerHouse premieres exclusively on Netflix in 2016!"

My phone immediately started blowing up with texts, alerts, and notifications. My friends were texting, "I knew it!" or, "The Gibbler is back!" News stories about the sequel (even with the very few details there were at the time) were spreading like wildfire. Fans' comments on social media ranged from, "Everything is right with the world again!" to the emotional spectrum of emojis (crying, laughing, heart eyes). The excitement was palpable, and it felt like a dream come true.

In a few short months, we were in production for season one of *Fuller House*. The first order of business was our initial table read, in which the actors gather around a table and simply read through a script so the writers can get a sense of which jokes are working and where the script needs improvement. Our first official table read took place upstairs in a big conference room in the writers' building. I had met Soni Bringas (who plays Kimmy's daughter, Ramona) a few weeks prior, but I was meeting the other kids (who play D.J.'s children) for the first

time. It all felt a little bit like the first day of school. I had butterflies in my stomach. I was meeting people with whom I'd be
spending a lot of time within the months, if not years, to come.

The table read included the first and second episodes; the
scripts had been delivered to my email inbox a few days prior.
That alone was a big change from the script routine all those
years ago on *Full House*. I still remembered the *thunk* of the
script being delivered to my doorstep back in those days. (How
old school!) I had read through both the first and second *Fuller
House* scripts at home several times, but I never actually said
my lines out loud until the day of the table read. I have no idea
why. Maybe I was afraid? Nervous? Maybe I needed the comfort of my costars to really get back into character? I don't
know.

But as soon as we started the table read, it all came right
back to me so naturally. Delivering my lines felt effortless. It's
like Kimmy Gibbler had never left my soul.

If the kids were nervous, they didn't show it one bit, despite
the fact that none of them had landed roles this big before.
Elias Harger, who was only seven years old at the time, completely stole the show. I just kept staring at him, in disbelief
that this little kid could time and deliver a joke like a thirty-
year-old man who had been doing this his entire life. He was
truly remarkable to watch. Jeff Franklin half-joked after the
read, "I think it took twenty years to remake this show because
we were just waiting for Elias Harger to be born."

It wasn't a perfect table read, but the chemistry was there.
We just needed to smooth out the kinks, which happens naturally as actors have more time to marinate together. Mark

Cendrowski (who is famous for directing almost every episode of *The Big Bang Theory* and happens to be one of Dave Coulier's oldest friends) was such a comforting, gentle leader. He acted as a mentor to the kids and reminded them that they need to "wait for the laughs." Mark was also great at giving us ladies really good direction without stepping on our toes. We did know our characters better than anyone, of course!

After our first table read came . . . our *second* first table read. Yes, you read that correctly: We actually had *two* first table reads. The initial read was small, with just main actors and writers present. Mark Cendrowski insisted on this to get us warmed up and comfortable in a more private environment. Our second first table read was the exact opposite of private: A massive, packed conference room full of cast, writers, producers, Warner Bros. executives, Netflix executives, and several strategically placed cameras for Netflix to capture this momentous occasion. Never in my life had I heard of a table read being filmed. We even had the hair and makeup team get us glammed up. No pressure, right?

That second table read was a lot more nerve-racking just because of the sheer number of important people in the room. My heart was beating a lot faster as we began this table read, but we quickly fell into a rhythm, and soon everyone in the room was laughing and it all felt like we were exactly where we were supposed to be.

Soon after the table reads, we visited the stage and saw the sets as they were still being built. When I walked through the living room set again for the first time in twenty years, the sheer force of all the memories could have knocked me right over. I was with Dave and Jodie, and no one spoke. The set had been built but not painted yet, so everything had a dull, monochromatic look, almost as though it had been covered with a thick layer of dust for the past two decades. Everything looked the same, yet different. It was like walking into your childhood home and feeling displaced yet also somehow comfortable at the same time. I had *so many* memories on this set. Was this really happening again?

We spotted framed pictures going up on the wall of the kitchen stairs and soon realized that these were actual pictures of *us*, as kids and now as adults, off the set at each others' homes or during trips we had taken together. In this strange world of televised fiction lived artifacts of a real family. How many shows can do that?

I also felt confused. I couldn't find the exit from the stage. The bedroom sets were on the opposite side from where they used to be, twenty years ago. We used to exit the kitchen alcove and walk directly into our craft service and makeup room. Now, the kitchen alcove was closed off and had been turned into a laundry room. What? It took me a few weeks before I could instinctively remember how to get to the (new) makeup room, or how to get back to our dressing room trailers (outside). Muscle memory is hard to retrain, I guess.

Our first week of work was not without speed bumps. We had two days of rehearsals and trying to get the show on its feet. On the third day—a pre-tape day, when the cameras are set up and we get into hair, makeup, and costume to pre-shoot scenes—something seemed amiss. Our ADs (Assistant Directors) were scrambling, and the shooting schedule for the day was suddenly turned upside down. What was going on? I realized that the schedule changes were made so that none of the scenes we were shooting involved the character Jackson, D.J.'s oldest son. At lunchtime, Jeff called for a powwow with the cast in the greenroom. He told us that the actor who had been playing Jackson had been let go. They were flying in the new Jackson from Florida that morning. Elias started crying.

We were all shocked . . . but the adults knew that this was not unheard of in the business. In fact, the role of Danny Tanner on the original *Full House* was initially played by John Posey before the role was recast and Bob Saget stepped in (the unaired pilot with John still lives on YouTube, in case you're curious to see the Danny Tanner that never was). The Jackson recast had nothing to do with the previous actor's skills. His acting was very good! He just didn't mesh with the other characters in the way the writers had hoped. Jeff blamed himself: "We miscast him. It's was our fault," he said. And to this day, the former Jackson's picture is still in one of the frames in the kitchen set at the back stairs. You would never know unless you were standing up close.

And so that was Michael Campion's entry into the show. His plane landed, he came to set, got a haircut, and started performing the very next day (which was our first audience show). What a welcome to Hollywood!

Our first audience show was unlike any other. There was an electricity buzzing in the air that we could feel in our bones. The audience greeted us with cheers that reverberated in our ears. They screamed each time a cast member appeared. They even cheered when the living room and kitchen sets were revealed. It's like those sets were another beloved character on the show, and everyone was so touched to finally see them in person again. Normally, when production starts on a new show, the actors and writers have no idea if the show will be liked by an audience. To know we were making a show that people were already so ecstatic about was a huge confidence boost. Our fans are simply the best.

I would be lying if I said I wasn't nervous for this first taping. My anxiety was in overdrive, and I was deep breathing and walking around outside in order to calm my nerves. When it came time to actually begin my first scene, though, I felt nervous but ready. The director called, "Action," and I walked up to the front door and turned around. Before I could even speak, the audience started laughing hysterically. *Wait . . . what are they laughing at?* I was so flummoxed by this unexpected laughter that I completely forgot my first line. Whoops!

Take two. I asked Gwenn, our dialogue coach, what the audience was laughing about. She pointed at me. I looked down and remembered I was wearing a classic Kimmy Gibbler outfit, complete with a scarf crocheted into bacon and eggs. I didn't even have to say a word; just the mere sight of Kimmy Gibbler was enough to make the audience chuckle. After all these years, I'm so used to my costumes that I forget just how outrageous they look to other people.

My return to Hollywood was exciting and heartwarming. We couldn't have asked for a better first season. Despite my anxiety, I felt very comfortable in this environment—literally the same set I had grown up on with (many of) the same people. It all felt very familiar, and I was very confident as an adult who not only had experience in the sitcom world, but life experience as well.

In contrast to our first episode, our last episode of season one was a doozy. It was an ambitious script involving a double wedding, where Kimmy runs and leaves Fernando at the altar . . . three times. And cake. The script called for me to eat copious amounts of cake.

We finished this monstrous episode, and the cast gathered for curtain call. Our adrenaline was surging; we could all feel it among each other. As the rest of the cast trickled out to the stage to take their final bows in front of a cheering audience, Jodie grabbed Candace and me and wrapped us up in a bear hug.

"We did it, girls. We did it," she whispered in our ears. "I am so effing proud of us." The moment suddenly became bigger than all of us. We finally understood with greater perspective just how special it was to have this opportunity again. As kids, we hadn't had the knowledge or life experience to fully appreciate just how rare it was to have an experience this extraordinary. Now? We couldn't be more grateful.

All three of us cried during that curtain call. Tears of pride and of happiness, not to mention gratitude that we were able to—if even for just this fleeting moment in time—capture that magic all over again.

The part I wasn't prepared for came after we wrapped our first season: Publicity. Returning to this business after twenty years off was a bizarre introduction to How to Be a Celebrity in the Twenty-first Century. During the early development of *Fuller House*, I distinctly remember walking back to our cars after one of our first meetings with Jeff and the writers. The topic of publicity came up, and how this first season of the show would be heavily publicized by Netflix, requiring a lot of appearances on our part. Candace happened to be on her way to a fitting with her stylist, and I inquired about it. She and Jodie advised me, "You will probably want to hire a stylist for our press events." Stylists weren't something we needed during the first run of the original show. I couldn't just dress myself?

They continued filling me in on details, such as how a stylist charges roughly $1,000 *per fitting*. When they saw my wide-eyed and silent expression, mouth agape, they were quick to reassure me, "Oh, but the stylist can usually do several looks per fitting." This did not reassure me as much as I think they were hoping. How many fittings would I need? *And you don't even get to keep the clothes after all that?* Maybe I was in the wrong business.

Candace and Jodie had to teach me everything about stylists and fittings and publicists and why I needed all this stuff in the first place. This wasn't really part of being an actor back when I was a kid and teenager. And now I was learning that it's basically a requirement. Where's that handbook on how to be a celebrity?

While I'm thrilled to be acting again, I would like to be upfront with you: I am a *terrible* celebrity. I'm not even entirely comfortable with that label: "celebrity." What does that even mean? If, for you, it conjures up an image of a beautiful, flawless actor confidently walking a red carpet, living in an extravagant house, driving the newest Tesla, and being adored by millions of fans around the world, then I am most definitely *not* a celebrity.

For starters, I am deathly afraid of red carpets. Doing interviews renders me panic-stricken. "Extravagant" living is also not in my wheelhouse. I bought my house, which I have lived in for sixteen years, because it was the cheapest one in my neighborhood in Orange County, where I grew up. No Hollywood for me! And my car—a sixteen-year-old Honda Pilot that doesn't have Bluetooth capabilities . . . or a working passenger-side lock, for that matter—is older than most of the kids on *Fuller House*. It is for sure the oldest car in the lineup of Porches, Audis, and Range Rovers outside our Warner Bros. Stage 24. But I drive it because it works. Why would I need a new one?

Same reasoning applies to my ancient iPhone. Several of my castmates, including Jodie Sweetin and Juan Pablo Di Pace, who plays my TV husband, constantly make fun of my tiny old iPhone.

"How cute!" Juan Pablo will say with a wink as he holds up my phone. "What are you up to now, an iPhone 2?" By now, I'm used to being teased about my dinosaur devices, and I stopped being defensive about them a long time ago.

My point? I thoroughly suck at this celebrity thing. The only reason I even remotely consider myself celebrity-*ish* is because I get recognized when I go out in public and have since I was a young kid. I have been giving autographs to strangers in malls since I was six years old. And now that I'm forty-three, it's all about the selfie! Selfies in Target. Selfies at the local nail salon. Selfies anytime I'm within two hundred feet of a school.

One time, I was in the drive-through of In-N-Out Burger, and the cashier walked out of the building and *got into the passenger side of my car to take a selfie with me*. I couldn't make this up if I tried! I visit this In-N-Out frequently enough that I'm used to the teenage cashiers fangirling out. But I would be lying if I didn't say that I was taken aback when this particular employee slipped into my car unannounced. The employee didn't knock or anything before getting into my car (because *knocking* would be weird). And it's not like my passenger-side door was locked because it no longer has that capability (see above).

You'd think this would be a highly unusual encounter (I mean, I'm not sure the employee's manager was thrilled), but for me it's just another day in my life: a selfie, fan questions, and "Can I get some extra ketchup with my fries, please?

One time, I was out to lunch with my college friend, Greg. Our server suddenly recognized me in the middle of our lunch. "Are you . . . are you . . . that girl from *Fuller House*?" he stammered. I replied that yes, I am. This poor kid got so flustered, he dropped a fork out of the pile of dirty dishes he was carrying, and the used fork landed right in my salad. Mortified, he apologized and offered to get me a new salad. Greg and I laughed about it afterward and left him a big tip. To this day, we joke that I need to get a tetanus shot before we have our annual lunch at this restaurant again.

Side note: One might also assume that celebrities get top-notch, A+ service at restaurants, but I've found the opposite to be true. More times than I can count, my order will end up wrong because the starstruck server is so distracted trying to figure out why I look familiar that they stop listening and write down my order incorrectly. I ain't mad; it makes me chuckle!

You may have noticed that celebrities often travel with a team of people to help them . . . do what exactly? Be a celebrity, I guess. Hair, makeup, stylist (all of whom make up the "Glam Squad"), publicist, and sometimes a manager or assistant or two. Holy hell. We can't even all fit in one elevator. Literally. Our first press tour for *Fuller House* in New York City required three large, black, luxury SUVs just to cart Candace, Jodie, and me and our "teams" around the city. And three elevator-car rides to get to the top floors of buildings. I was so embarrassed. No one outside of the president of the United States should require such a large entourage!

All of this was very overwhelming to me, the kid who had been out of show business for twenty years. Had the business really changed that much since I left? Or had *I* changed? Maybe it was both. Either way, it was a massive culture shock.

At the super-important Netflix 2016 Winter Television Critics Association (TCA) press extravaganza, a mere six weeks before our new show was set to premiere to the world, five of us sat on a panel in front of a couple hundred television critics: Candace, Jodie, creator Jeff Franklin, executive producer Bob Boyett, and myself. I felt like I was sitting in front of a firing squad. *Full House* had never been popular with critics during its heyday, and here we were, all these years later, attempting to explain the spin-off of that show to people whose job was to be critical.

Gulp.

I was determined not to remain silent during the entire panel. "Come up with a few sound bites you want to convey," a Netflix rep had advised us beforehand. *I can do this*, I thought.

The first question out of the gate: "What was it like when you saw the *Full House* set for the first time again?"

I forgot about my plan and piped right up. "It was like . . . walking onto an archaeological site that had just been unearthed after twenty years."

Cringe. What does that even *mean*? I guess I was referring to that monochromatic layer of dust the set appeared to have, but *man* that visual did not come out of my mouth the way I wanted it to. Talk about word vomit!

It was too late. I couldn't recover. My phone started blowing up because every critic was posting this awkward sound bite on their respective media outlets' Twitter accounts.

I stayed silent for the rest of the panel.

It wasn't all terrible, these press tours and junkets. I have to admit that, even in spite of my anxious terror, we got to participate in a lot of really cool opportunities. We got to act out a *Full House* skit with Jimmy Fallon on *The Tonight Show*, where the set dressers had replicated Michelle Tanner's bedroom right down to the pencil bed. Jimmy Fallon was *such* a cool, down-to-earth guy. It felt like he was just as excited to do this skit as we all were.

We also got to be guests on *Ellen*, which was beyond fun. She has the nicest staff backstage, swag for the visiting talent (Ellen undies, anyone?), and really creative games and skits. There is an energy on her set that is infectious. The first time I sat on her couch I was in awe, excited, and super nervous. But

Ellen was as personable in person as she appears on TV. She asked us about what it was like being back on the *Full House* set before showing a clip of exclusive scenes from the yet-to-be-seen season one. It was our first time seeing the new show on the big screen, and we all squealed! At the commercial break, I reached over to the Ellen mug in front of me to take a sip of water, then hesitated. I wondered if this was prop water just for show, or if it was water meant for drinking.

"Is this real water?" I asked Ellen.

She laughed. "No, we only use fake water on our show!"

Candace and Jodie explained to her that I had been out of the business for two decades, so I was a little slow to catch on. Ellen paused and looked at me.

"You haven't done this in twenty years, yet you can do *that*?" she said as she pointed to the big screen, where (as Kimmy) I had just done my MC Hammer Time dance, punctuated by my "All that and a bag of chips! You go, girl!" line. I blushed.

"Yeah," I sheepishly replied.

"I'm impressed!" Ellen nodded. Now I was squealing secretly on the inside. What a compliment from the comedian extraordinaire herself!

Returning to the spotlight also forced me to confront my own body. I don't normally consider myself to be super conscious of my body. (Note: not self-conscious, but *conscious*— meaning I don't usually think about my body on an everyday basis.)

But there is something about being an actor that suddenly makes you hyperaware of every physical flaw you have. That may seem super obvious—DUH! I'm on TV with millions of people watching! But it's not that, so please hear me out.

"The Fitting" is something that I worry about quite often. It probably seems glamorous to get to try on dozens of outfits and shoes—and sometimes it is. But on the regular? I don't love it, because the fitting forces me to look in the mirror at my body and how clothing fits (or doesn't fit) for long periods of time. And I think, over time, that would make anyone hyperaware of every curve of their body.

It has nothing to do with anything anyone has ever said to me. Our costumers are outstanding at what they do, building up our confidence and making sure we're comfortable. Our producers never say a word about how we're supposed to look. This is all me and my issues.

I just want to look great and wear comfortable, flattering looks. And we always eventually get there! But the process of getting there (i.e., The Fitting) reminds you of what doesn't fit and what doesn't look good on you. You gotta go through the bad to get to the good.

Think of the last time you went swimsuit shopping, or shopping for a nice dress to wear to a wedding. If you're like me, you leave the fitting rooms feeling mostly frustrated until you find the one thing that works. Now imagine going through those motions every day as part of your job.

I've mentioned previously my dislike of red carpets. They stress me out for weeks beforehand. I have always assumed that my discomfort was due to my inexperience. But it's been almost five years of red carpets, and my feelings have not changed. Why? I've had some time during the writing of this book to ponder this question, and here's what I've concluded.

On a red carpet, you get one chance at *the* photo. You know that this one photo will be out there on the Internet for the world to see and access forever. And we, as a culture, have made it a pastime to critique red carpet looks, for some reason. Lists of Best Dressed and Worst Dressed. Recap shows. Entire magazine issues devoted to breaking down how people look on a red carpet. Whether the review is positive or negative, we have made this into a thing.

Why do we do this as a culture? Why *is* this a thing? I hate this practice. I wish we would stop making it a form of entertainment. It makes me super uncomfortable, and I think I've finally pinned down why: A red carpet is a single snapshot of time. It is a single snapshot that is then used to form an opinion about a person. It is *literally* a snapshot. And there are many times, in fact, when I read comments and opinions that mirror my own insecurities about myself. It is a visual, written confirmation of the negative chatter in my head.

And it can be crushing.

That single snapshot really doesn't tell you anything about me. It tells you what I'm wearing and whether I'm having a good hair day. But it does not tell you even a fraction of who I am. I have so much value that I bring to this world, so many qualities that I'm proud of. I'm smart AF. I write with passion. I am a devoted friend. I am a fiercely loving mother. I am funny as hell, both on- and offstage. I am honest, and I connect to people. I am brave and unafraid to talk about my flaws.

Do you see *any* of those things in a single snapshot on a red carpet? NO.

The red carpet photo is such a wholly incomplete picture of who I am. It might show you that I ate too many Girl Scout cookies that month. It might show you that I cut my hair. It might show you that I have a penchant for A-line silhouettes.

But it really doesn't show you anything about me that is worth discussing.

Speaking of looks, the cast of *Fuller House* in particular hears comments regularly like, "You never age!" or "You must be drinking from the Fountain of Youth!" These compliments are very, very kind. But I fear that comments like these lead people to value youthfulness over aging, and that leaves me feeling uncomfortable. I'd prefer if everyone knew that I've lived a full life that I'm very proud of, and if my age *does* show (and it does), that's a good thing! Age has brought wisdom and perspective and confidence. My age spots show that I've spent a lot of time running outside in the sun (even with sunscreen!) and enjoying life outdoors. The crow's-feet in the corners of my eyes are markers of all the years I've spent laughing. My not-so-perky boobs are reminders that I nursed two children during those sweetest of baby years. My expanding waistline shows that I've enjoyed a lot of delicious food and, on many occasions, the world's best margarita (at El Cholo in Southern California—order the Cadillac!).

I'm so much happier and more confident now than I ever was as a smooth-skinned twenty-year-old. Aging is not something to be afraid of. I'm okay with aging and looking older.

And when I do need to cover those age spots? I'm lucky enough to have a wonderful makeup artist who knows all the best tricks. When it comes to Hollywood, let's not forget to remember that it takes a village.

So that's a pretty big change from child stardom twenty years ago to now. Another difference between then and now—and something reporters have regularly asked Candace, Jodie, and me about—is the fact that we have gone from supporting roles to lead roles. But, to be honest, one of the biggest differences has simply been the transition from child actor to adult actor. (No mandatory school hours! We can drive ourselves! We can be a lot more opinionated about the storylines!)

I guess being a lead doesn't really feel that different because *Full House* always felt like an ensemble show, and in many ways the sequel is, too. The show is about the family in and around the house. They call us three ladies "leads" because we bring with us recognizable characters and a built-in audience. In that sense, we do carry the show. But the kids and the supporting players are just as valuable and integral as anyone else.

A reporter once insinuated, during an interview that was heavily about the Olsen twins, that I must be really glad that the Olsen twins chose not to come back because now I have a lead role. I guess he was suggesting that I *wouldn't* have this large of a role if Michelle was back in the house? It's funny, I actually never thought of it like that.

When Jeff came up with the idea of *Fuller House*, he approached me long before "Will the Olsens come back?" was even a question. He always had the idea of D.J., Stephanie, and Kimmy being the lead adults who raise D.J.'s three boys. As you recall, this is a flip of the original series—where Danny (dad), Jesse (uncle), and Joey (best friend) raise Danny's three daughters. In fact, I would argue that having Kimmy as one of the three is even *closer* to the original premise than it would be having Michelle. It was never three brothers raising the girls, and it's not three sisters raising the boys. Regardless, I'm forever grateful to be part of the show in any capacity.

I have always been confident that Kimmy Gibbler can hold her own as a character. She is very clearly defined, and she's well loved by our audience (although, in some cases, people love to hate her!). My costars are so, so, *so* incredibly good at what they do, I never felt pressure as one of the leads of the show. Everyone adds value and talent, and what you get is an exceptional team with killer chemistry.

The area in which I do feel pressure as a lead is representing the show offstage with the interviews (the bane of my existence!) and publicity. It's a pressure we never had as kids. It's a pressure we felt a lot before the show premiered in 2016. *What if it all flops? Will it be on our shoulders? That we couldn't bring this wonderful thing back to life?*" (I felt less panicked after we completed the first two seasons and the fans keep wanting more.)

I want to make sure that I am always representing our show to the best of my ability. I want to give thoughtful responses and honor the legacy of the series. I don't want to just "gossip." I want to give fans tidbits, but also talk honestly and seriously about a show that means the world to me. For all the horsing around and crazy antics that we do on the show, we take it very seriously.

And in yet another example of, "Wow, things sure have changed over the last twenty years," I had to do a lot of soul-searching and a lot of advice-soliciting before I hired a publicist. It actually took me a full two years to do so! I saw publicists hanging around frequently at press appearances, but I couldn't figure out their purpose in physically being there. They seemed to be on their phones a lot, or fetching water and snacks for their celebrity when necessary. Tell me again why I needed to hire one?

I finally decided to swallow my pride and ask for help. I met with Candace's managers, Ford and Jeffrey, who have been working with her for most of her career. When this wild ride started with our new spin-off show in 2015, Candace graciously told Jeffrey and Ford, "Whatever Andrea needs, do it for her." So there I was in 2017, sitting with them in their office, swallowing my pride, and asking questions that basically belong in *Hollywood for Dummies*. (Come to think of it, maybe I should write that book, too.)

What's the difference between an agent and a manager (or a publicist, for that matter)? Do I really need all of these people? What would you do if you were me?

Their answer surprised me, although maybe it shouldn't have. They told me to hire a publicist. Really? But I hate publicity! Why would I pay someone to make me do more of what I hate? Jeffrey not only recommended a particular publicist to me, he also assured me that she would help make me more comfortable with this entire crazy-making process. And do a lot more than get me water and snacks.

And you know what? He was right. Alegra, my publicist, has

been a godsend. She turns down requests that make me apprehensive. She finds press and opportunities that fit into *my* wheelhouse instead of trying to fit me into a world that makes me wholly uncomfortable. She makes sure I feel safe on the red carpet and cuts off the line of interviews when I've reached my max or become overwhelmed. She knows me and my boundaries, and she helps create a happy and healthy work environment for me. That truly is priceless.

Side note: How classy was it for Candace to be so willing to share her managers and their talents with me? And how classy was it that Ford and Jeffrey not only freely and willingly gave me their time (several hours over several meetings) and advice, they didn't try to snag my business for their own benefit? This is what grace and friendship look like, people. I may not love this whole "celebrity" title, but I sure am grateful to have friends who are willing to help me. I truly love acting and my *Fuller House* tribe, and if participating in doing press is what it takes to return to the parts I love, I'm willing to learn. I just need a hand to hold from time to time.

I feel very fortunate to have been given the chance to return to Hollywood, no matter how bumpy the road can sometimes be. It's an opportunity that many people only dream of, and I don't take that fact for granted. Every single day, no matter how long or stressful a day it's been, I feel grateful when I walk through the stage door. To be given these opportunities and work with my lifelong friends and make millions of people laugh and enjoy the "comfort food" that is *Fuller House* . . . well, I couldn't have scripted a better return to acting.

CHAPTER TWELVE

My "Full House" Family

IT'S A BEAUTIFUL, PICTURE-PERFECT sunny day in Southern California in May. I'm sitting in a lounge chair on the lawn of Jeff Franklin's home in Beverly Hills with a stunning panoramic view of Los Angeles. Felicity is snuggled in on my left, and Michael is sitting to my right. We're eating vegan sliders and seven-layer dip and drinking margaritas (virgin for Felicity!). As I look out over the backyard, I see Jodie trying to convince her daughter, Bea, who jumped into the pool fully dressed, that it's time to dry off. Candace and Lori are chatting and laughing next to the food tables. Michael Campion and Soni Bringas are engaged in a highly competitive game of Ping-Pong. Elias is screaming down the waterslide and splashing around with his real-life siblings and John Brotherton's two little girls. I see Fox and Dashiell (who alternate playing Tommy) gleefully swimming down the lazy river with their floaties on. Bob Saget and his fiancé, Kelly, come over for a hug and to share news about their upcoming wedding. And in the middle of it all, Jeff is beaming, basking in the glow of being surrounded by the family he created thirty years ago, a family that keeps growing in size and love each year.

I feel a contentment that's hard to explain. My history with each one of these people is unique, but fulfilling. The newer cast members I've only known a few years, but we still feel like an extended family. The original *Full House* cast members I've known three quarters of my entire lifetime. How lucky am I to have had them in my life for decades? To have grown together instead of apart? To be closer now than we were even back then? How incredibly fortunate are we to get to do this all over again?

My relationships with John, Bob, Dave, and Lori have changed a bit since I was a kid. I'm an adult now, with my own lifetime of experiences—both good and bad—under my belt. And because I have new perspective, I appreciate them more now. I have always loved them and looked up to them, and they have always made me laugh. But my love and respect for them has only grown. Now Candace, Jodie, and I are the leaders and mentors on the show. And we couldn't have had better role models than John, Bob, Dave, and Lori to pave the way for us. They taught us how valuable it is to have close relationships with the kids on the show. They taught us the benefits of having constant laughter on set. They embraced us as kids and showed us the love of a family. And that has returned to us a hundredfold. I am so grateful to them, and for their continued presence and love in our lives. And they still make me laugh like no one else!

Dave—both then and now—has always been the best at cracking a joke when things on set drag on too long or the director is tense because he can't get a shot. Last season, Dash kept running offstage in his cute little waddly, toddler way instead of staying on his mark and doing what the baby wrangler was trying to get him to do. "Action!"—cue Dash running offstage. It was like clockwork. So on the fifth or sixth take, the director called action and *Dave* ran off the stage, perfectly mimicking Dash's toddler stomp. I laughed so hard. We really, truly needed that comic relief, and we can always count on Dave to provide it!

Dave has always been known as the joker on the set, but *Fuller House* brought the chance for him to try his hand at directing for the very first time. He directed the "Nutcrackers" episode, which of course immediately prompted a dozen silly jokes about the title. (What a perfect title for Dave!) But once he got the title out of his system, he settled down and got straight to work. He prepared for weeks for his directorial debut. He shadowed his good friend, director Mark Cendrowski. He sat in on table reads and network meetings. He took this job as seriously as I've ever seen him take anything. I thought the week he directed would be filled with fart sounds and funny voices, but boy, was I wrong! Watching Dave work as a director is the most serious I've ever seen my funny friend.

As it turns out, Dave is one of the best directors I've ever worked with, and I'm not just saying that because we're so close. He is the perfect actor's director. He gives great notes and suggestions, but still makes you feel like you're in control of your character. He empathizes with you as an actor. I had a mini breakdown during the "Nutcrackers" episode because we had rehearsed the final Rat King death scene *so many times*. I had even gone to private dance rehearsals with the dance company in order to nail this scene. And yet, after every run-through, Jeff Franklin asked for *more*. More death. More dancing. More Michael Jackson moves. I ended up doing the Gibbler Gallop, MJ choreo, the shopping cart, disco moves, and two deaths, *and* I kicked another dancer in the nutcracker . . . and Jeff's response was, "Let's hire a professional breakdancer." *Are you flipping kidding me?* I was at my wit's end. I was working my ass off, and the only feedback I was getting was, "Not enough. Let's bring in a professional."

This is where our friendship and trust in one another really shined through. Dave let me vent to him as much as I wanted. He validated my feelings. He told me to let Jeff do what he wants and hire a breakdancer, to trust the process. And you know what? He was right. Jeff eventually nixed the breakdancer idea. He liked what we were doing. And come tape night, the audience howled with laughter! I think Dave directing me as an actor brought us even closer.

As for my other closest friends from the show, Candace and Jodie are my soul sisters. I love them unlike anyone else outside of my real family. Growing up on the set of a sitcom is an experience that is very different from that of most other children. And since that sitcom was *Full House*, it felt special, unique. As kids, we felt cared for. We felt important. We felt like family. It felt less about the business and more about the bond.

For this reason, among many others, I have always said that Candace and Jodie are the only two people on this earth that can really understand my childhood. There were other child actors in the '90s, sure, but no one else can relate to what it was like to specifically grow up on Stage 24 on the Warner Bros. lot. It shaped us as kids. It's a part of the makeup of who we are today.

So here we are, thirty years later, sharing an even *more* unique experience as adults playing the same roles we created as kids, on the same set, on the same stage—but this time with a world of experiences and kids of our own. It is just as cool and wonderful and cherished and mind-blowing (if not more so) as it appears to the outside world.

We are *almost* back in our same dressing rooms. We moved up—into Bob, Dave, and Lori's dressing rooms!

The thing that has changed the most is our gratitude. It's fun, sure—it's always been fun. But the experience this time around, as adults, is so much more meaningful. We know how fleeting this is: the business, friendships, life. We don't take it for granted. We know each other incredibly well. I can tell when Candace is having a rough day. Jodie knows exactly the right thing to say. Jodie knows what triggers my anxiety. Candace knows how to mend the hurt. We are rhythmically entwined in a way that is unlike any other friendships I have ever experienced.

The success and legacy of the show is our priority. But what ranks even higher is our friendship. Our sisterhood. I love these women. They drive me absolutely bonkers at times, like when Jodie makes me watch ridiculous YouTube videos in between scenes, or when I catch Candace doing squats and flexing before scenes. But I love them fiercely and will champion them every day. They are my heart and soul.

Candace and I are even closer now than we were as kids. It's ironic that we played best friends on *Full House*, but it wasn't until the series ended that we became so close. Candace became a willing ear when I was deep in the throes of my divorce. Because I felt ashamed, I hadn't told many people about my divorce back then. Candace was trying to set up a time when I could make an appearance on one of her shows. I kept delaying and ignoring her . . . until I finally came clean and told her that, as much as I really wanted to be a part of her show, I was in the middle of a divorce and trying to set up custody and time-sharing between my kids and their dad. I was too overwhelmed to commit to anything outside of my personal life. Without hesitating a single moment, she said she understood completely and dropped the topic of the show appearance. She gave me advice and was there for me when I needed to share what I was willing to share, and she provided a good distraction when I simply wanted to get my mind off of all my troubles.

She was, and still is, a super fun friend to hang out with. We don't need or want glamorous parties or to rub elbows with other celebs. We're happiest staying in, sharing a bottle of wine, and laughing until the wee hours of the morning. One time we stayed up late, me tipsy-tweeting Jonathan Knight from NKOTB. (And he responded to me!) Candace put socks on my feet and tucked me into one of her spare beds (her sons were gone on a hockey retreat that weekend) and said good night. That Deej really is the ultimate good friend.

Candace gets a lot of attention in the press for her conservative religious beliefs, and I think people assume I am *not* conservative or religious and may wonder about our friendship. It is true that our politics are opposite, but the way I see it is this: We have far more in common than we have differences. Our friendship is greater than our differences. And I love her even when we disagree.

One highlight of our shared time together during the twenty-year hiatus between shows was our first NKOTB concert together. We went with a group of friends and screamed like teenagers all night. We met some of the band members after the show (Candace had met them before, but it was my giddy first time). Someone snapped a picture of just Candace and I together, and the next thing I knew, the photo went viral and appeared on every online media source. Oh, Mylanta! Even though we had kept in touch all these years, this was the first real photo evidence of seeing "Kimmy and Dccj" back together again. And people went *nuts*. There was something about two former TV best friends from a hit '90s show attending the concert of a '90s band that sent fans' nostalgia into overdrive. And thus, a hashtag was born: #BFFgoals.

One of our favorite pastimes, however, is being active together. Although we don't manage to work out together often, we are the ultimate complement to each other at the gym: She is all about strength training, and I am all about cardio/running. This led to us somehow committing to one of the toughest obstacle mud courses in the world: Tough Mudder. Three miles (which felt like ten) and twenty-five obstacles, all in the mud after a rainy morning in Malibu. What could be more fun than that? Although it was incredibly challenging, the camaraderie of our team was our strongest force. We crossed the finish line on a complete endorphin high.

It was on the early-morning bus ride to the Santa Monica Mountains for this Tough Mudder in 2011 that Candace and I first discussed just the tiniest hint of a *Full House* spin-off. *Girl Meets World* (the sequel series to the hit '90s TV show *Boy Meets World*) had recently premiered.

I mentioned it to Candace. "Why can't we do something like that? It would be so fantastic!"

Candace just shrugged. (I can't remember exactly what she said.) John Stamos had attempted to put together a reunion movie several years earlier . . . which was met with a not-so-enthusiastic response from people, including some of the cast-mates. I had just given birth to Felicity at the time of John's proposal. I was feeling all postpartum-y and out of sorts, so at that time, I wasn't keen on the idea of an official reunion. Putting on neon tights again, but with my postpartum mommy body? No way. We quickly forgot about it as the bus arrived at the muddy starting line of an epic Tough Mudder course, and we didn't talk about it again until years later.

As I've mentioned previously, there were several years during *Full House* when I was closest to Jodie out of the entire cast. We related to each other and laughed a lot. After the show ended, we went our separate ways and didn't see much of each other. There was nothing wrong or amiss—we just grew apart for a time. I suppose we needed to each grow in our own directions and find our own paths . . . and eventually, to each fight our own demons. There was a long period of time when I simply didn't hear from Jodie at all, only piecing together later that this was the time in her life when she was struggling with addiction. We fell out of touch, and she didn't respond to emails. I don't know what it's like to go through addiction and rehab specifically, but I know what it feels like to battle with horribly difficult life issues. And I know that we *all* have a past; we have all struggled to varying degrees. The important thing is how you come out of it. I choose to see someone *not* as the sum of their worst parts, but as the best version of themselves. And what I see in Jodie are all her best qualities as a good mother and a strong, deeply loyal, fiercely confident woman.

Today, Jodie is the person that the kids flock to on set. She is the "fun" mom who also knows how to command respect. When the kids are misbehaving on set, they will listen to her when she "moms" them (discipline is too harsh a word for Jodie's style). She frequently invites the kids over for playdates and swim parties at her house. She is fun, yet she knows when it's time for business.

Jodie is the person who is always coordinating fun outings for the cast and crew, much like John and Bob did for us back in the *Full House* days. She is like the social director on set. This can be anything from an intimate cast dinner after an appearance, or a twenty-five-plus-person group outing to a shooting range. She loves her friends and is fiercely loyal. If you are considered a good friend of Jodie's, you are family.

Jodie and I had some epic frenemy story lines in the original

Full House, like when Kimmy offered to pierce Stephanie's ears. There was something about our banter that delighted our audience to no end.

The same holds true today. When we have our annual pre-season meeting with the writers each year, they always ask, "What do you want to see more of?" And Jodie and I always reply, "More Stephanie/Kimmy bits! We love our bits!" And it's true. When Jodie glares at me in character and I lob an insult her way, there is nothing more satisfying. We have a chemistry that is very special, both on- and offscreen. And I think the audience can feel it, which is why they respond the way they do.

A highlight from season four is what I've dubbed "The Jodie Prank" and will go down as one of the best pranks in Stage 24 history. One rehearsal day, Jodie took a Sharpie pen and autographed all of the props sitting on a table, thinking they were giveaways for fans in the audience that week. (One of our weekly traditions is to sign extra, unused props and give them away as prizes.) Little did she realize that they were the *actual* props for the entire show, which we were getting ready to run through for the studio and network any minute. We teased her relentlessly about it! "Jodie, don't sign this!" became a common phrase around the stage. Jodie retaliated by signing a hundred sticky notes and pasting them to my dressing room door. Then *I* retaliated by printing up two hundred T-shirts with her autograph—one for every member of our cast and crew. She showed up for work one day and the entire cast and crew were waiting for her in the living room set, gleefully wearing the shirts with her autograph largely displayed on two hundred chests. *Checkmate, Jodie.* (You can watch this entire prank on my YouTube channel!)

One of the things I love most about our show is that the weird hierarchy among cast, crew, producer, and assistants doesn't really exist on our stage. From what I've been told, on most other shows there is very little "commingling" between "above the line" employees and "below the line" employees. (Even just these phrases make me cringe.) Our collective team at *Fuller House* blurs, or even erases, that line.

I care deeply about my hairstylist, Sandy, and my makeup artist, Farah. One of my favorite parts of each week is sitting in their chairs so that we can catch up on each other's lives. We call it "hairapy hour" (a play on "therapy hour"). Sandy tells me about what her sons are up to post-college. Farah gives me the latest gossip about her roommate and her hot neighbor down the street. I ask for their advice about everything from parenting teenagers to how to get a pimple to disappear overnight. There is an intimacy that exists between us—the actress and the glam team. Farah knows every single one of my blemishes, sun spots, and other facial flaws. It's not even something I'm insecure about with her; I trust her to make me look my best. Sandy is someone I can be 100 percent honest with about what hairstyles I'm hating that day. They both instinctively know when I need quiet to focus on learning my lines, or when I would rather have distracting levity in the room. They are invaluable to me.

I know the same goes for Candace and Jodie, too. One of our favorite memories from our shoot in Tokyo was a night after we had wrapped for the day and gone out with our ADs, (assistant directors) Chris and Adam, to participate in a traditional Japanese activity: going to a karaoke bar! We managed to find one of the smallest karaoke bars in all of Tokyo and somehow had the place all to ourselves. It was awesome to see Chris and Adam (who are two of the hardest-working people on the set—they are the glue that holds everything together) let loose with a mic in hand. Chris did a killer word-for-word rendition of Vanilla Ice's "Ice Ice Baby." Candace and I belted out New Kids on the Block's "Step by Step." Candace rapped a flawless version of Sir Mix-A-Lot's "Baby Got Back." Adam took videos of it all, and we could not have possibly had more fun. By the end of the night, a local Japanese couple quietly sat at the table next to us. The man recognized us and asked for a photo. Fueled by sake, we invited him to sing a karaoke song with us. Well, whaddya know . . . the *Full House* theme song was in the booklet of karaoke offerings. So you know we just had to sing it with this polite young man! It was a moment that you could not have scripted, and will probably never be replicated.

It has become our annual tradition, started by Jodie and our Netflix executive, Teddy, to go to Universal Halloween Horror Nights every October. Should it be weird that we are commingling with a top Netflix exec who could very well influence the outcome of the show? The thought doesn't even cross our minds because we're too busy screaming at the goblins and laughing at how ridiculously terrified I get in these damn horror mazes. I am a walking target for these zombies, screaming with my head buried tight into the chest of Teddy's husband,

Larry, who has become my unwitting protector at this annual scare fest.

I love this tribe. We are all working toward one goal: to make a kickass (family) show. But also to laugh and love each other while doing it.

One thing that delights me to no end is seeing our children—who are the same ages that we were growing up on the set of *Full House*—play together and forge their own friendships. Jodie's daughter, Zoie, and my daughter, Felicity, are only a year apart. They love to hang out in our dressing rooms on tape night and play, making music videos together or creeping down to the schoolroom on set or the kids' dressing rooms to see what they are doing. Jodie's younger daughter, Bea, is a few years younger than Zoie and Felicity, and she loves just trying to keep up with the "big girls." It's funny when I see the three girls together; it reminds me a lot of myself, Candace, and Jodie as kids.

During season two, Zoie and Felicity had the opportunity to be extras on an episode of *Fuller House*. The script had Max's third grade class doing school presentations in the Fuller backyard, and the show needed kids around the same age to fill in as the classmates. So this was Felicity and Zoie's chance to be in their moms' shoes for a day or two.

It was a surreal, full-circle moment to be driving my daughter to Warner Bros. at 5:30 A.M. on a Thursday pre-tape day. I thought, *So this is what it was like for my mom to drive me to set every day for all those years.* Felicity struggled a little with the 7 A.M. call time but never complained because she knew this was such a unique and special opportunity. I also tried explaining to her that she was lucky to be getting some perks that the other background performers wouldn't get, like being able to hang out in my dressing room instead of the common area where the background performers would wait. The concept of nepotism was probably too big for her to grasp at her age, but I was proud to see that she fully understood her luck and didn't take it for granted.

When we arrived on set, we laid out the clothes we'd brought, and one of our costumers came by to help select an outfit for Felicity to wear. Then it was time for her to go rehearse her scenes while I stayed back in my room to learn my lines for the day. I wasn't in any of Felicity's scenes, so we were on opposite schedules. I wouldn't be on camera until later in the day.

One of the ADs brought work permits for Jodie and me to fill out for our daughters to legally allow them to work on set. After a few minutes, I heard Jodie call out from across the hall, "Hey, A.B.! Do you know how to fill this out?" I laughed. I was struggling at that very moment with the exact same problem. Our moms had always done this for us when we were kids; we had no idea how to fill out work permits! We laughed and joked that we should call our moms to help us.

Later, we made our way down to the backyard set to watch the girls tape their scenes. Unbeknownst to us, our hair and makeup team had given Felicity and Zoie a little mini-glam touch-up and curled their hair and put lip gloss on their lips. How sweet is that? I watched them tape the scene from the director's monitors. I could see exactly when Felicity was on camera, and I found myself iterating a stage mom–esque internal monologue: *Look alive! You can't yawn. You never know when you'll be on camera! Pay attention!* Oh, dear. It was hard for me to watch without wanting to mentally correct her. I needed to relax and get a grip! Fortunately, those "stage mom" thoughts went away quickly, and I was able to enjoy watching my daughter experience life on set and take direction from the director (who happened to be Joanna Kerns of *Growing Pains* fame that week).

They ended up giving Felicity a little "feature" bit where she, playing a student, displayed her classroom project to the class, which was a windmill made entirely out of Barbie dolls. Felicity was instructed to spin the windmill blades and then take a short bow. At one point, they even tried to give her a line—to say "thank you" as she was taking a bow. But I guess she performed the line a little *too* well and started air-kissing like she was accepting an award. The extras are supposed to *blend in*, not upstage the actors! So they decided to cut the line. (I actually hate the term "extras," as I think it sounds a little elitist. Truth be told, I really respect the work of extras on a show, since it's a thankless, but essential, job.)

The pre-tape day was a long day—Felicity worked the full eight hours that she was allowed to work by law, according to that pesky work permit. At the end of the day, I asked her, "So what did you think?"

"It was cool," Felicity began. "But kinda boring, too. There's a lot of just sitting around and waiting." Yup, that's Hollywood, kid. It's not all glamorous!

They taped the same scenes in front of an audience the next night. I think Felicity was a little nervous with a full studio audience there, but her dad, brother, and grandparents were all in the audience, which thrilled her. At the end of the night, there was one perk left that Jodie and I actually requested—to have our daughters walk out with us during curtain call so we could all take a bow together. It was a very special moment for all of us, and one I will never forget. The last thing I wanted before we wrapped up this whole experience was to get a picture of Felicity, my mom, and me on the famous blue *Full House* living room couch. *Now* everything had truly come full circle.

Candace, Jodie, and I are all very different from one another. In some ways, we couldn't be more different (outgoing versus shy; Hollywood savvy versus very unsavvy). But we have never felt more bonded than we do today. The She Wolf howl we do on the show is a little hokey, but that connection is real. Last year, Jodie gifted me and Candace personalized gold rings engraved with the words "She Wolf." And just like in the Japan episode, we really do plan on getting tattoos to symbolize our unique friendship. (We just need to decide on a design. I'll get back to you in a few years on that one!)

We grew up as children of the '90s, so we understand, like much of our audience, the pull of nostalgia. I think every generation longs for their childhood, but the nostalgia for the '90s seems particularly strong. Dr. Jean Twenge says that this is because "the '90s were, arguably, the last good decade—the last time the economy was doing pretty well and the last time we weren't worrying about terrorism. Many millennials experienced a '90s childhood of peace and prosperity, only to enter adulthood during the Great Recession. It's like someone baited and switched them. So going back to the '90s seems especially appealing to them."

Bringing *Fuller House* to life, while retaining the same loving family values as *Full House*, has been particularly satisfying because of this power of '90s nostalgia. We don't take ourselves too seriously on *Fuller House*, and we fully acknowledge that our brand of comedy is silly and oftentimes involves outlandish scenarios. But at its heart, it's about love. It's about family. It's about a definition of family that includes *all* the people you love, not just those who are biologically related.

We hear from fans quite frequently that they wish they had been part of a family like the Tanners and their tribe. *Full House* felt like home—a very large home with a lot of people living it in, but home nonetheless, with a close, tight-knit family. When we traveled to Japan to do press for season three, one Japanese reporter told us that multigenerational families living under one roof is common in Japanese culture, which is why she thinks *Fuller House* resonates so well with Japanese citizens.

I think that's the appeal of our show. We represent more than just the conventional family with a mom, a dad, and 2.5 kids. And hopefully, the show appeals to people who grew up motherless or fatherless, to families with same-sex parents, to people who were raised by aunts and uncles instead of moms and dads, and to single parents, widows, and widowers.

After all (cue the sappy music here, but I mean this), the entire premise of *Full House* is that there is no one definition of family. "Family" is the people who love you.

At the end of the evening at Jeff Franklin's house, we wrangle the kids out of the pool and all gather together on Jeff's porch for a toast and a speech. Jeff talks about how proud he is of each of us, how proud he is of the show and what we have created together. I look around our gathered circle and see so many generations of kids, and kids' kids. Families come in all shapes and sizes; every family looks different, and this one is mine. It is big and inclusive and wonderful. With full glasses and full hearts, we toast to one another.

CHAPTER THIRTEEN

Curtain Call

I'M IN MY BED, right in the middle of those sleepy twilight moments, that in-between state of being not awake yet not asleep. I'm smiling in my post-celebratory margarita buzz after hearing the wonderful news that *Fuller House* has been picked up for season five.

My phone vibrates; it's a message from Candace: "Season five will be our final season."

Gut punch.

This is news that I knew would eventually come one day. But I still felt like I'd had the wind knocked out of me. We had already said goodbye once, after eight seasons of *Full House*. And then we were given the unexpected gift of getting to do it all over again. I feel really lucky. And a little heartbroken that it's ending . . . again.

I woke up the next morning, and those words—"final season"—came flooding back into my consciousness. I felt that familiar wave of depression mixed with anxiety.

What will I do now? Will I ever feel this fulfilled again? Will

I continue to pursue a career in acting that I never expected I would have as an adult? Or will I, once again, fade into obscurity and enjoy a more private life?

I've thought a lot about these questions, and I still don't have a clear answer. The future (and the business) is unpredictable, and I don't know what opportunities will be available to me in a few years. Will I have more opportunities thanks to the connections I've made through *Fuller House*? Will I be typecast? Will I struggle to find work as an aging woman in Hollywood? I don't know the answer to any of these questions.

On the screen, you see a comedic actress giving a no-holds-barred performance, often involving a bizarre assortment of stunts, physical gags, singing, or dancing. What you don't see is a woman who still continuously questions if she is in the right profession, despite people telling her all her life that this is her calling.

If I am so good at comedic acting, why does it sometimes feel so at odds with my mental health?

It's a question I still struggle with to this day. I don't know the answer. I know that I enjoy a private life. I know that my heart calls me to advocate and speak out for mental health awareness and empathy. I know that I love to write. I know that I love to make people laugh. I know that I love to run. These are the absolutes; everything else is a big question mark.

In the last few years, I have often felt that it doesn't really get better than this for me. I work with the best people in show business. Our set often feels like a three-ring circus with all of the animals, kids, stunts, and crazy costumes. For the Halloween episode during season two, we had 4:00 A.M. call times to get into makeup (Jodie and Adam's zombie makeup alone took four hours), followed by a sixteen-hour workday, only to come back twelve hours later and do it all over again. Our crew is there long before the actors arrive and stays long after we wrap. We have the hardest-working crew in show business: Twenty minutes after curtain call, our crew is already tearing down old sets and building new ones for the next week. And yet, despite the circus, everyone returns year after year. They say it's because of the people—it truly feels like an extended family on Stage 24. I love this show and the legacy it has left of good, comforting, loving, family programming. If I stayed in this business, would I still love it as much as I do now?

If I had to make a quasi-prediction, I would say I could easily see myself teaching acting to middle school students. I think I'd find that kind of mentorship experience very rewarding. I could just as easily go back to work in study abroad and traveling a lot once my kids are older. I could also see myself writing children's books about kids who feel like they don't quite belong.

I don't know what the future holds. What I do know is that I am lucky to have experienced many lifetimes' worth of experiences. I never take my life for granted. Even the darkest times of my life . . . I'm grateful to have experienced those lows. I've gained an arsenal of knowledge and confidence as a result. Those experiences made me who I am today.

My whole life has come full circle. I'm back where I started, but I'm nothing like the person I was when I began. My life experiences have made me a more complete human being.

The show will soon be over. But the people will never leave my life. My castmates. My She Wolf sisters. They will be a part of my life until my final breath—that is the one thing of which I am most certain. And our fans! Our fans will continue to support us, long after the stage lights have been turned off. New fans will be born, and new generations will be introduced to this wonderful family show that has and will continue to encourage parents and kids to watch television together for decades to come.

In that sense, *Full House* and *Fuller House* will live on forever in our hearts. Every time a child hears, "How rude!" for the first time, or attempts to replicate the Gibbler Gallop, new life will be breathed into our show. It will live on forever in our collective memories.

I will think about all of these things when I stand on the doorstep of the Tanner home for the very last time. I'll be standing in the exact same spot, literally, playing the exact same character as I did more than thirty years ago. But the little girl then and the adult that I am now are worlds apart. I know how to identify and manage my anxiety now. I discovered new passions. I accept things about myself that I previously hated. I have experienced heartbreak and pain. I have a teenager of my own now.

The director will call "Action!" and I'll step through the front door one last time, just like I've done hundreds of times before. And I know I'll feel a peace that I've waited for my entire life.

My heart is full.

Why the World Needs Kimmy Gibblers

AFTER THE SEASON THREE PREMIERE of *Fuller House* at the Paley Center last September, a fan came up to me and said, "Thank you for teaching me it's okay to be weird."

That comment stuck with me. For eight years on *Full House*, Kimmy Gibbler was the butt of many jokes. The Tanners routinely screamed in terror at her sudden appearance at the kitchen back door. In one episode, Stephanie subtly called Kimmy a "horror" after Kimmy gives her a copy of Madame Kimmy's Horoscope column in the school newspaper. "A horoscope?" Stephanie replies. "What's that, Kimmy? A telescope that can only see *your* face?"

I used to simply chalk it up to Kimmy being the comic relief of the series. It's just comedy! Kimmy Gibbler is a punch line! It is only recently that I have begun to see the true value in being weird.

It's easy to buy into the "be like everyone else" mentality. It's safe, it's comfortable. The road to normal is well paved and well populated. But being weird and standing out? *That* can feel like a solitary trail. It's hard being different, especially during those formative years. We live in fear that someone will reject the very traits that make us peculiar.

I am nothing like the character I play on *Fuller House*. I'm shy and introverted, and I prefer to blend in. But feeling different and strange? That's something I can 100 percent relate to. My childhood was unusual in that I didn't really fit into the Hollywood scene, but I never felt like I quite fit into the normal high school scene, either. As you now know, I still feel similarly displaced when I step onto a red carpet in full-blown panic at the hundreds of strobing flashbulbs but need to act like I can effortlessly maintain an air of confidence. Where *do* I belong?

By contrast, and despite the thinly veiled insults hurled her way, Kimmy never wavers in her bold confidence. She continues to wear bright colors, polka-dot overalls, and mismatched patterns. She continues to barge through the kitchen door unannounced. She continues to lob one-line comebacks to her naysayers with the surety of a tennis player acing a serve.

Kimmy Gibbler exemplifies the one maxim we all should embrace: Be yourself. It's a kind of self-love and unwavering confidence that is rare in teenage girls. Kimmy Gibbler has it in droves.

When Ben Platt won a Tony Award for his performance in 2017 as the anxiety-ridden teenage lead role in *Dear Evan Hansen*, he concluded his acceptance speech with a special message to young people: "Don't waste any time trying to be anyone but yourself, because the things that make you strange are the things that make you powerful."

The Evan Hansens (and Kimmy Gibblers) of this world are not only being heard, but being *celebrated* for their differences. The offbeat characters, normally relegated to sidekick roles, are now being promoted to lead roles *and* being honored and respected—flaws, imperfections, weirdness, and all.

What does this say about our audience?

People are seeing qualities of themselves in these characters and responding with overwhelming appreciation. To see aspects of one's psyche—parts of yourself that you've kept quiet or hidden for decades—play out on a public stage is both validating and eye opening. You discover parts of yourself that you didn't know were there. You accept parts of yourself that you previously rejected. You realize it's okay to be weird. Strange *is* powerful.

I received a tweet from a fan just recently that perfectly sums up why the world needs more Kimmy Gibblers. A Twitter user named Jeffrey wrote to me, "I'm glad your character exists because you make being different amazing. I was bullied a lot growing up, and Kimmy made me feel good to be different. I would love to meet someday and give you a hug and say thank you."

Oh, Jeffrey . . . thank *you*.

Being weird isn't about being outlandish. It's about having the courage and confidence to be who you were born to be.

Be brave. Be yourself. Love others. Laugh often. The world needs more of this.

ACKNOWLEDGMENTS

To Kelley, my therapist for over a decade, who helped me write this book without even knowing it. You showed me the pathway to a better, healthier life and proved to me that life is worth waking up—and fighting—for every day. You gave me the tools to build a better life. You lit a fire inside me that inspires me to help others with similar struggles. My gratitude for you is boundless.

To Jeremy and Kelli, who shaped my story in ways that I didn't necessarily want or expect. But you have showed me the power of kindness and grace even in the most unusual of circumstances. Thank you for redefining what it means to be "family" in an all-inclusive way that makes our kids feel more loved than ever. I appreciate you more than you know.

To my running friends: Lily, Cathie, Laurie, Eileen, Danna, Pavey, Chris, and so many others whom I don't have room to name . . . you are badass runners who inspire me to get outside and be a better version of me. You accept me without judgment when I don't perform to the best of my abilities. You inspire me to be a better runner, but more importantly, you inspire me to be a better human. Because you can't be one without the other.

To Doc, for always believing in my intellect and abilities even when I doubted myself. I am a better, more well-rounded, and worldly person because of you.

To Joe, Jordan, Jonathan, Danny, Donnie, and my Blockhead sisters—A2, Angela, Katie, Jared and Julie: Thank you for creating a happy space in which I could sing and dance to my heart's content and, ultimately, escape from the stressors of life even for just a brief moment in time. Nostalgia is a powerful antidote to almost any challenge or grief.

To Melissa Coulier, for creating a cover photo for this book that perfectly captures the spirit of my story. I love you and your brilliant mind. Credit or debit!

To Rennie Dyball. You have become one of my greatest mentors and a life coach more times than I can count! And most of all, you are a confidant that I knew from the very beginning I could trust without hesitation. I simply could not have done this without your guidance and gifted talent. Your instincts, writing, and editing are unparalleled; however, it is your uncanny ability to connect with others that is your greatest gift. I cherish our time together. Thank you for helping me bring this dream to life.

To the rest of my book team: My agent, Katherine Flynn, my editor, Denise Silvestro, and the rest of my Kensington family. Thank you for seeing me, really *seeing* and believing in me and my vision for this book. From our very first phone conversation, you understood me, my passions, my vulnerabilities, my talents, like no one else. Thank you for believing in my ability to bring not just an entertaining book to the bookshelves, but a book that can make a difference in people's lives. That is the kind of work that I hope has a lasting effect on our readers long after they finish the last page of this book.

To April, who understands grief, healing and the power of second chances unlike anyone else. Your friendship, your openness and honesty, and your ability to make me laugh has healed me (and I believe each other) a hundredfold. Our training runs together remain some of my fondest memories. Thank you.

To Greg, who hugged me through every heartbreak and wrote to me when I needed to hear your words more than ever. You have shown me what it means to be a true friend, and I can only hope that I can grow to be as dedicated a friend to you as you have been to me.

To Ellen, my forever BFF. My fondest memories of high school are with you. You filled my teenage life with endless laughter and joy that only our Taco Bell Thursdays and *Beverly Hills, 90210* could do. You have always treated me as a best friend no matter what stage of life, with or without fame. I can forget to call you for way too long, and yet when we both pick up the phone it feels like two puzzle pieces coming together. Thank you for your unconditional friendship.

To John, Bob, Dave, and Lori. For accepting me into the family from day one and creating a set environment in which I could feel so welcome and loved. Any and all accolades we have received for *Fuller House* are really because YOU set the example of how to lead a show with love, humor, and family at its core.

To Jeff. Thank you for this life you have given me. You have changed my life in profound ways simply by never ceasing to believe in my ability to make people laugh. You put so much of yourself into this show, and I hope you remember that its success is because of you. All of the memories we have created and the extended family we have built are because of you. You will forever be the heartbeat of *Full(er) House*.

To Candace and Jodie. You are the closest thing I have to sisters. You understand and accept me exactly the way I am. You make me laugh like no one else in this world, yet I spontaneously cry thinking about all of the blessings we have shared together in this short lifetime. You are my She Wolf Pack, forever. That bond is unbreakable, and long after we take our last curtain call and the lights dim on the *Fuller House* set for the very last time, my love for you will outlast everything else.

To the *Full(er) House* fans! Thank you for your unwavering loyalty to the show. YOU are the reason we were able to bring that magic to the screen all over again. Bringing the character of Kimmy Gibbler to life (again) was an absolute highlight of my life. Thank you for sharing with me the ways in which Kimmy impacted your life.

To my brothers, Darin and Justin, for keeping me in check, giving me grief about my long showers, and keeping it real. I love you guys with my whole heart . . . even though I'm still Mom's favorite. :)

To Michael. For showing me that I can be accepted and loved no matter how many flaws I possess. For helping me believe in love again. For loving my children and filling a hole in my heart that I thought would never feel whole again. I love you, even (especially) when you are a curmudgeon. You are forever my MH.

To my parents, who gave me life in more ways than one. You nurtured me back to health when I was in crisis. And I know you would do it again without hesitation. You taught me what it means to be an unconditional, selfless parent. My greatest hope is that I can be the same kind of rock to Tate and Felicity as you have always been for me. I love you.

To Tate and Felicity. Being your mother has been the greatest joy of my life. Just when I think my heart is full, you grow and make me proud and prove that my heart has no boundaries when it comes to loving you two. You have made my life complete. There are no two people on earth that I love more than you . . . even when you complain about my cooking and refuse to clean your rooms. Thank you for being the reason I smile every day. I love you with all of my soul.

Connect with Us

Visit us online at
KensingtonBooks.com
to read more from your favorite authors, see books
by series, view reading group guides, and more.

Join us on social media

for sneak peeks, chances to win books and prize packs,
and to share your thoughts with other readers.

facebook.com/kensingtonpublishing
twitter.com/kensingtonbooks

Tell us what you think!

To share your thoughts, submit a review,
or sign up for our eNewsletters, please visit:
KensingtonBooks.com/TellUs.